THE JEWISH
GARDENING
COOKBOOK

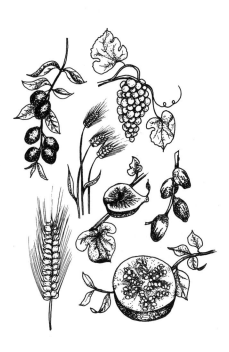

THE JEWISH

GARDENING

COOKBOOK

*Growing Plants
and Cooking for
Holidays and Festivals*

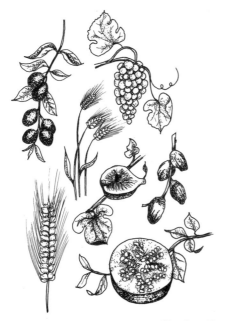

by Michael Brown

Illustrated by
Laura C. Martin

Jewish Lights Publishing
Woodstock, Vermont

The Jewish Gardening Cookbook
Growing Plants and Cooking for Holidays and Festivals

Grateful acknowledgment is extended to: Oded Borowski, for translation and interpretation of the Gezer calendar as originally featured in *Agriculture in Iron Age Israel: The Evidence from Archaeology and the Bible* (Winoma Lake, Ind.: Eisenbrauns, 1987); Cherry Lane Music Publishing Company, Inc., for reproduction of *The Garden Song,* words and music by Dave Mallett, copyright © 1975 Cherry Lane Music Publishing Company, Inc. (ASCAP)/DreamWorks Songs (ASCAP), worldwide rights for DreamWorks Songs (ASCAP) administered by Cherry Lane Music Publishing Company (ASCAP), all rights reserved, used by permission; David Hendin, for permission to reproduce the ancient coin photos that appear on pp. 19–20, photos copyright © David Hendin, reprinted with permission; and to Howard Schwartz, for permission to reproduce "The New Year for Trees," copyright © 1977 by Howard Schwartz, all rights reserved.

Library of Congress Cataloging-in-Publication Data
    Brown, Michael P., 1956–
    The Jewish gardening cookbook : growing plants and
cooking for holidays and festivals / by Michael Brown.
        p.   cm.
    ISBN 1-58023-004-0
    1. Vegetable gardening. 2. Food crops. 3. Food. 4. Fasts
and feasts—Judaism. 5. Cookery, Jewish. 6. Bible. O.T.—
Quotations. I. Title.
SB320.9.B76 1998
635—dc21   98-10721
                                                           CIP

First Edition
10 9 8 7 6 5 4 3 2 1
Manufactured in the United States of America
Book design by Sans Serif, Inc.
Jacket design by Molly Cook Field

Published by Jewish Lights Publishing
A Division of LongHill Partners Inc.
Sunset Farm Offices, Route 4
P.O. Box 237
Woodstock, Vermont 05091
Tel: (802) 457-4000 Fax: (802) 457-4004
www.jewishlights.com

Contents

PREFACE

The idea for this book has evolved over a long period of time. About eight years ago my family and I returned to America after spending close to ten years in Israel. Like every other family that moves, we had our own personal considerations. Life in America is, of course, very different from that in Israel. There is good and bad in both countries, and we made our adjustments.

One of the things I missed most about Israel, however, was the land. I missed walking the countryside and feeling the sense of history. I missed feeling the connection between the landscape and the vegetation with the history of the Jewish people. And I missed the realization that the same types of trees and herbs and flowers I was seeing everyday were those same plants that our ancestors had experienced.

In short, I missed the bond between the land and myself as a Jew.

In America I knew I couldn't reproduce this feeling, but perhaps I could re-create hints of my feelings from there. At the same time, the fact that I was outside Israel made me strive to establish new links between the land and myself (and my Jewish identity) that were not previously important for me.

So, part of this book is about conjuring up old images, and part is about creating new links. As an avid gardener, I feel most at home doing this in my garden. We can certainly be thankful for God's gifts whether we live in Israel, Indiana—or, for that matter, even in Istanbul.

To my wife Nurit,

who has shown me the beauty and vitality

in our Jewish tradition.

ACKNOWLEDGMENTS

This book began as a series of unrelated activities revolving around planting, harvesting, and celebrating the Jewish holidays. As the idea for a book crystallized, two friends in particular were instrumental in encouraging me to pursue the project. I would like to thank Howard Stern and Alan Brown, who constantly spurred me on with their excitement regarding the ideas in this book and the manuscript itself.

Rabbi David Eligberg of Congregation B'nai Tikva in North Brunswick, New Jersey, kindly devoted time to answering many of my various esoteric questions.

Creating a book is never an easy activity. Research, writing, and promotion all demand great deals of time. I thank my wife, Nurit, and our three children, Maoz, Noam, and Keren, for their patience, encouragement, and understanding regarding my time constraints during this period.

I was lucky enough in my search for an illustrator to find Laura Martin. Her easygoing manner and cheerful flexibility have been greatly appreciated. Her detailed botanical illustrations have greatly added to the beauty of the book.

Without Jewish Lights Publishing, this book would not have been produced. I would like to thank sincerely several members of the staff with whom I have had direct contact. Though I don't know many of the other staff members by name, I also wish to thank all those who work behind the scenes in bringing a book to fruition. This is a team effort involving many people. Specifically, Stuart Matlins, the publisher, helped me develop my rough ideas into a coherent manuscript. His many valuable suggestions are felt throughout the book.

Arthur Magida, my editor, was "just an e-mail away." His expertise, help, and reassurance were always welcome. Lastly, but certainly not least, I want to thank Jennifer Goneau, associate editor. She is the one who has so carefully taken care of all the many details that are so important in the production of a book, and that are so easily put off or forgotten.

INTRODUCTION

RHYTHM OF THE JEWISH CALENDAR

A season is set for everything, a time for every experience under heaven:
A time for being born and a time for dying;
A time for planting and a time for uprooting the planted;
A time for slaying and a time for healing;
A time for tearing down and a time for building up;
A time for weeping and a time for laughing;
A time for wailing and a time for dancing;
A time for throwing stones and a time for gathering stones;
A time for embracing and a time for shunning embraces;
A time for seeking and a time for losing;
A time for keeping and a time for discarding;
A time for ripping and a time for sewing;
A time for silence and a time for speaking;
A time for loving and a time for hating;
A time for war and a time for peace.
—Ecclesiastes 3:1–8

Jewish life has a rhythm. Just as the Jewish week is dominated by the Sabbath, so too is the Jewish year dominated by a cycle of holidays that take us from planting time to harvest. The Jewish calendar is the tool that keeps all the holidays in their proper seasons. It is based on the movement of the moon around the earth. A lunar month (the time it takes the moon to circle the earth) is a little more than 29½ days. A lunar year comprises 354 days—about eleven days less than a solar year.

Because of this shorter lunar year, the Jewish holidays

occur about eleven days earlier each year. If this pattern were to continue year after year, the holidays would eventually float around throughout the seasons. Imagine if Passover fell in the winter. According to the Bible, the grain harvest should be gathered during the second day of the holiday, but there would be no grain. At Shavuot there would be no first fruits of the season to offer at the Temple, and at Sukkot there would be no harvest to celebrate.

To keep the holidays more or less in the seasons called for them in the Bible, an extra month is added to the Jewish calendar approximately every three years (actually, seven times in a nineteen-year cycle). In the days of the Second Temple, the Sanhedrin, which was the supreme judicial body in Jewish life, was responsible for setting the calendar. The Sanhedrin sent agents into the countryside each year to check the condition of the crops and the livestock. Lambs, which needed to be slaughtered for Passover, had to be grown sufficiently for this. Also, the barley had to be ready for harvest on the second day of the holiday. After discussion among themselves, they would decide whether or not to add an additional month to the calendar. Placed before the month of Nisan, it was called Second Adar.

Eventually, mathematical principles were used to determine this additional month. By the middle of the fourth century C.E., the Jewish sage Hillel II had written the principles that are still used today for establishing the calendar.

In 1908 the archaeologist R. A. S. Macalister discovered the earliest known Jewish "calendar" during his excavations in Palestine of the ancient city of Gezer. Dated to around 925 B.C.E., this small limestone slab consists of seven lines listing agricultural tasks to be performed at specific times of the year. According to the translation of the calendar by Oded Borowski, in his book *Agriculture in Iron Age Israel,* the agricultural tasks are:

Two months of ingathering (or harvesting) of olives

This would include the time allotted for pressing of the oil.

Two months of sowing (grains)

During this time, farmers planted wheat and barley.

Two months of late sowing

During this time, farmers sowed legumes such as peas and chick peas.

A month of hoeing weeds (for hay)

This is often translated as a month of hoeing flax or harvesting flax with a hoe.

A month of harvesting barley

This was celebrated with the festival of Passover.

A month of harvesting (wheat) and measuring (grain)

This is also translated as harvest and festivity, and harvest and finishing. This period ended at approximately the time that Shavuot began.

Two months of grape harvesting

A month of ingathering (of summer fruit)

This would include such fruits as figs and pomegranates.

AGRICULTURE IN ANCIENT TIMES

If, then, you obey the commandments that I enjoin upon you this day, loving the Lord your God and serving God with all your heart and soul, I will grant the rain for your land in season, the early rain and the late. You shall gather in your new grain and wine and oil.
—DEUTERONOMY 11:13–14

Jews of biblical days were intimately tied to the land. They interacted with it everyday. From the produce of their fields they received their livelihood. When they gave thanks for their produce, it was a personal thanks. They depended on the harvests for their existence.

The Bible is full of information about the daily life of the Israelites, and modern archeology has supplied important

xvi • THE JEWISH GARDENING COOKBOOK

additional information. When the Israelites entered the Promised Land, they could not immediately drive the Canaanites out of their fortified coastal cities. Instead, they settled the Judean hill country and the arid Negev. In the Bible we read of the Israelites' difficulty in trying to settle the surrounding hills, and of Joshua's exhortations for them to do so. Their first task while doing this was to clear the forest to create farmland:

> "If you are a numerous people," Joshua answered them, "go up to the forest country and clear an area for yourselves there, in the territory of the Perizzites and the Rephaim, seeing that you are cramped in the hill country of Ephraim." "The hill country is not enough for us," the Josephites replied, "and all the Canaanites who live in the valley area have iron chariots, both those in Beth-shean and its dependencies and those in the Valley of Jezreel." But Joshua declared to the House of Joseph, to Ephraim and Manasseh, "You are indeed a numerous people, possessed of great strength; you shall not have one allotment only. The hill country shall be yours as well; true, it is forest land, but you will clear it and possess it to its farthest limits. And you shall also dispossess the Canaanites, even though they have iron chariots and even though they are strong." (Joshua 17:15–18)

Through the necessity of farming in the hills, the early Israelites perfected the technique of terracing. In the flat coastal plains there had been little need for this type of cultivation. But in the hills the Israelites used it to create agricultural land in an area difficult to cultivate.

PLANTING FOR FUTURE GENERATIONS

In keeping with their attachment to the soil, our ancestors thought also to plant for future generations, as the following story suggests.

Emperor Hadrian was marching with his troops to fight a province which had rebelled against him. On the road, he encountered an old man who was planting fig saplings. Hadrian asked him, "How old are you now?" When the old man replied, "A hundred years old," Hadrian said, "You are a hundred years old, yet you go to all this trouble to plant fig saplings! Do you expect to eat from them?" And the old man said, "My lord emperor, I am indeed planting. If I am worthy, I shall eat the fruit of my plantings; and if not, then even as my forebears have labored for me, so I labor for my children." After spending three years at war, Hadrian returned and found the old man in the same place. What did the old man do? He took a basket, filled it with beautiful first ripe figs and presented it to Hadrian, saying, "My lord king, pray accept this from your servant. I am the same old man whom you found busy planting saplings on your march. Behold, He who is everywhere granted me the privilege of eating the fruit of my saplings. The figs in the basket are some of that fruit." Hadrian ordered his servants, "Take the basket from him and fill it with gold coins." His servants did so, and the old man took the basket filled with gold coins and went home. (Leviticus Rabbah 25:5)

WITHERING OF AGRICULTURAL TIES

Through the centuries the fate of the Jews has been a roller coaster of opportunity and despair. Many countries enacted laws limiting the rights and freedoms of their Jewish citizens, and frequently Jews were barred from land ownership. The picture of the wandering Jew arose from the rootlessness of the Jew who was forced to wander from country to country in search of opportunity and security. Over the years most Jews became estranged from the land. Nowadays, when all professions in most countries are finally open to Jews, the occurrence of a Jewish farmer, even outside the Land of Israel, is rare indeed. Instead of praying for rain for our crops, we hope for a sunny day for our barbecue.

Agricultural connections to the holidays have withered

and been displaced by other meanings that are more under-standable to us. While these newly acquired meanings are cer-tainly legitimate and meaningful, we should not forget other significant meanings associated with our holidays.

Passover, with its rich agricultural roots, has been almost totally engulfed by the story of the Exodus. Shavuot has fo-cused on the giving of the Torah. Even Sukkot has lost much of its agricultural relevance. Without a connection to growing things, we miss out on some of the essence of our religion.

THE JEWISH GARDEN

GARDEN SONG
BY DAVID MALLETT

Inch by inch, row by row
Gonna make this garden grow
All it takes is a rake and a hoe
And a piece of fertile ground.

Inch by inch, row by row
Someone bless these seeds I sow
Someone warm them from below
Till the rain comes tumblin' down.

Pullin' weeds, pickin' stones
Man is made of dreams and bones
Feel the need to grow my own
Cause the time is close at hand.

Grain for grain, sun and rain
Find my way in nature's chain
Tune my body and my brain
To the music from the land.

Plant your rows straight and long
Temper them with prayer and song
Mother Earth will make you strong
If you give her love and care.

Old crow watchin' hungrily
From his perch in yonder tree
In my garden I'm as free
As that feathered thief up there.

Gardening has been called one of the most popular leisure time activities. Most of us, at the very least, grow a few plants or flowers to beautify our living areas.

Perhaps you're asking, "What is a Jewish garden?" Though it is essentially a collection of plants, it's really more than that. You don't just grow plants in a Jewish garden; you incorporate them into your life. Some will help transport you to distant times and places; others will provide your senses with aroma, taste, and beauty. All will help you experience a more personal attachment to God and to Judaism.

You can call this "hands-on-Judaism": growing something with your own hands, watching it grow and develop, flower and fruit. As this is happening, you become more cognizant of God's world—the temperature, rainfall, wind, and soil, and all the elements that go into growing plants. Little things such as these (and that we ordinarily overlook every day) become important to us as gifts of God.

Produce that we have grown ourselves simply cannot be compared with what we purchase from a store. "Our" produce has a history. We planted and nourished it; we watched it through all its stages of development. "Our" flowers somehow look brighter, smell more fragrant. "Our" vegetables and fruits are juicier, tastier, and better looking.

Through gardening we are given so many more

opportunities to thank God. When we taste the first fruit of each tree or vegetable, the *shehechiyanu,* which is the prayer of thanksgiving said when doing something for the first time or for the first time in the present season, gives us a simple, direct way to interact with God. Because we went through the whole process—sowing, tending, and harvesting—the "thanks" means so much more than it would for produce that has been grown by someone in a different state, or even halfway around the world.

With our Jewish garden the year takes on a whole new meaning. Instead of living in our world, dominated as it is by the secular calendar, we can begin to see a rhythm develop within the Jewish year as it revolves around our Jewish garden. Perhaps you will notice that Passover heralds the fresh spring growth or that Rosh Hashanah is a particularly good time to plant your garden.

In your Jewish garden you can explore and reach out to conventions to which you may be unable or unwilling to commit yourself. For example, even if you are not *shomer shabbat,* a Sabbath-observant Jew, instead of spending Saturday hoeing and weeding, sit in your garden on Saturday and enjoy its sights and fragrances.

If you haven't had a garden until now, this is the time to consider it. You don't need acres of land or even a large plot. Some of the nicest gardens are small, intimate collections of a few carefully chosen plants.

GROWING AND USING THE SEVEN SPECIES

For the Lord your God is bringing you into a good land, a land with streams and springs and fountains issuing from plain and hill; a land of wheat and barley, of vines, figs, and pomegranates, a land of olive trees and [date] honey; a land where you may eat food without stint, where you will lack nothing; a land whose rocks are iron and from whose hills you can mine copper. When you have eaten your fill, give thanks to the Lord your God for the good land which was given to you.
—Deuteronomy 8:7–10

The Seven Species, *shivat haminim* in Hebrew, are described in the Bible to illustrate the fertility of the Land of Israel. They include some of the most beautiful plants growing in Israel, and certainly some of the most useful. Though some are more "popular" than others, they all figure prominently in our history and literature.

FIG (*FICUS CARICA*): A SYMBOL OF PEACE AND PROSPERITY

And they shall beat their swords into plowshares
And their spears into pruning hooks.
Nation shall not take up
Sword against nation;
They shall never again know war;
But everyone shall sit
Under their own grapevine or fig tree
With no one to disturb them.
for it was the Lord of Hosts who spoke.

—MICAH 4:3–4

The fig tree must have made a strong impression on our ancestors. References to figs and fig trees appear frequently in the Bible and Jewish folklore. In fact, the fig tree seems inseparable from the Land of Israel. Their large leaves have shaded the weary, and their sweet fruit, eaten fresh or dried, has sustained generations of travelers, farmers, and ordinary folk. The tree was especially valuable in ancient times because its fruit does not ripen all at once, and is therefore available over a long period of time.

In Jewish tradition many scholars identified the fig as the forbidden fruit in the Garden of Eden. Much of the association stems from Adam and Eve using fig leaves to clothe themselves, as Genesis 3:7 says, "Then the eyes of both of them were opened and they perceived that they were naked; and they sewed together fig leaves and made themselves loincloths." This idea is also illustrated in the following parable:

> A king's son disgraced himself with one of the maidservants. When the king heard of it, he deprived his son of high rank and expelled him from the palace. The son then went about to the doorways of the other maidservants, and none would take him in. But she who disgraced herself with him opened the door of her house and received him. So, too, when Adam ate of that tree, the Holy One deprived him of lofty status and expelled him from the Garden of Eden. Adam then went about among all the trees, but none would receive him. But the fig tree whose fruit Adam had eaten opened its doors [so to speak] and received him. (Midrash Genesis Rabbah 15:7)

The fig tree is used often as a symbol of peace and prosperity. The quote that opens this chapter is perhaps the most famous example of this. In I Kings 5:5 this idea is expressed again. It perfectly captures the feeling of well-being that must have existed during the time of King Solomon: "All the days of Solomon, Judah and Israel from Dan to Beer-sheba dwelt in safety, everyone under his own vine and under his own fig tree."

In rabbinic literature the fig tree is compared numerous times to the Torah. Each of the following three examples emphasizes a different attribute of the fig and, therefore, of our relationship to Torah.

> Why is the Torah likened to a fig tree? Because the fruit of most trees, such as the olive tree, the vine, and the date palm, is gathered all at once, while the fig tree's fruit is gathered little by little. So it is with the Torah. One studies a little each day and eventually learns much, because the Torah is not to be learned in one or even two years. (Midrash Numbers Rabbah 21:15)

> With the fig tree, the more one tends it, the more figs one finds on it. So it is also with words of Torah: the more one studies them, the more morsels of wisdom one finds in them. (Babylonian Talmud, Eruvin 54 a–b)

> Why is Torah likened to a fig tree? Because all other fruits contain useless (inedible) matter. Dates have pits, grapes have seeds, pomegranates have rinds. But the fig, all of it, is edible. So words of Torah have no worthless matter in them. (Yalkut, Joshua, tract 2)

In the book of Jeremiah, the prophet has a vision in which the Jewish people are compared to figs:

> The Lord showed me two baskets of figs, placed in front of the Temple of the Lord. This was after King Nebuchadnezzar of Babylon had exiled King Jeconiah, son of Jehoiakim of Judah, and the officials of Judah, and the craftsmen and smiths from Jerusalem, and had brought them to Babylon. One basket contained very good figs, like first-ripened figs, and the other basket contained very bad figs, so bad that they could not be eaten. And the Lord said to me, "What do you see, Jeremiah?" I answered, "Figs—the good ones are very good, and the bad ones very bad, so bad that they cannot be eaten."
>
> Then the word of the Lord came to me: Thus said the Lord, the God of Israel: As with these good figs, so will I single out for good the Judean exiles whom I have driven out from this place to the land of the Chaldeans. I will look favorably, and I will bring them back to this land; I will build them and not overthrow them; I will plant them and not

uproot them. And I will give them the understanding to ac-knowledge Me, for I am the Lord. And they shall be My peo-ple and I will be their God, when they turn back to Me with all their heart.

And like the bad figs, which are so bad that they cannot be eaten—thus said the Lord—so will I treat King Zedekiah of Judah and his officials and the remnant of Jerusalem that is left in this land, and those who are living in the land of Egypt. I will make them a horror—an evil to all the kingdoms of the earth, a disgrace and a proverb, a byword and a curse in all the places to which I banish them. I will send the sword, famine, and pestilence against them until they are ex-terminated from the land which I gave them and their fore-bears. (Jeremiah 24)

FIGS IN THE GARDEN

Fig trees are versatile outdoor plants. They make a striking focal point in any garden. In cooler climates, they also add a touch of the tropics to the yard. In warmer climates, where winter care is minimal, they can even be arranged as a small grove. However you use them, their smooth gray bark and large lobed leaves are always attractive, and their delicate fragrance is inviting to all who venture near. Sitting in the shade of your trees, gazing at the fruit in various stages of de-velopment, you can imagine yourself in a different time and place.

Varieties/Purchasing

Many different varieties of figs can grow in your garden. Some do best only in hot climates; others are suitable for cooler weather. Ask your county agricultural extension agent which are best for your conditions. The agricultural extension agent is part of a nation-wide network of government experts re-sponsible for, among other things, agricultural education. They can usually be found in your telephone book's listing for county offices.

If you have room, grow several varieties to determine which are best suited to your area. Several standard mail-order catalogs have one or two varieties of figs. Some specialty catalogs list more than a dozen or so different varieties. See the appendix at the end of this book for a selective listing of these companies.

By nature the fig is a sub-tropical tree. However, a number of varieties can be grown in climates having cold winters and growing seasons as short as 6 to 7 months. In warm, humid locations, it is best to consider a variety with a relatively closed eye, which reduces spoilage due to outside elements. The eye is the small opening at the end of the fruit. Following are descriptions of some of the more common varieties of figs.

Alma: A new variety released in 1974 by the Texas gricultural Experiment Station. The greenish-brown fruit is average-sized and very sweet. It requires a long, warm season to ripen. The tree is very frost sensitive, especially when it is young.

Brown Turkey: Medium-sized light-brown fruit with a mild sweet flavor. The eye is moderately closed, and the tree is vigorous, large, and productive. This variety produces a fair crop on young growth, and is relatively resistant to cold.

Celeste: Small pear-shaped, light-brown to violet-bronze fruit with pink pulp and very sweet flavor. The plant is vigorous and large. The fruit is resistant to souring and splitting. The eye is tightly closed. The tree is resistant to cold.

Green Ischia: Also known as "Verte." This is a small, relatively hardy tree that produces fruit with excellent flavor. The fruit remains green when ripe, which makes it harder for birds to recognize.

Kadota: This is a large, vigorous tree with yellow-green fruit. It does best in warmer climates, which is why this is the variety grown commercially in California. It has a few, very large early figs, followed by a main crop. The fruit is especially good for canning or preserving.

Site/Planting

Fig trees do best in an area with a long, hot, and dry growing season. In less-than-ideal climates they will benefit from a sunny southern exposure against a fence or wall, which will also offer some protection from wind.

Even though figs do best in mild climates, they will tolerate quite a bit of cold. When fully dormant, the trees are hardy into the teens. At colder temperatures the tree will die back to the ground, but will resprout the following spring. This means that all of the tree that is above ground will die. New growth will originate from the roots, which will remain alive.

Actually, in order to fruit, fig trees do need a certain amount of cool weather. They have a chilling requirement of 100 to 300 hours below 45°F. In other words, they must be exposed to 100 to 300 hours (depending on variety) of temperatures below 45°F.

Figs prefer rich soil with good drainage. If you live in an area with heavy clay soil, try planting your trees in a raised bed or a mound. During the time immediately after planting, water regularly and mulch well, at least 4 to 5 inches. For mulch I use grass clippings or straw, but other materials are fine. Keep grass and other plants at least 2 feet from the tree. Figs have an extensive system of shallow feeder roots, many of them just under the surface of the soil, and plants around the base of the tree will compete for nourishment. The tree should grow vigorously. Under favorable conditions you can expect as much as 3 to 5 feet of new growth the first year.

Depending on the climate, variety, and growing method, fig trees should be spaced from 8 to 25 feet apart. Shorter spacing is more appropriate for potted plants and for smaller trees growing in cooler areas.

Routine Care

Figs need little attention during the growing season. Keep them mulched to reduce weed competition and preserve moisture. Your main job will be to thin out growth. Eliminate branches growing into the center of the tree, and branches growing into each other. Cut or pull out suckers sprouting from the roots of the tree.

Though figs are drought tolerant, they appreciate an occasional deep watering. In fact, for best fruit production, watering is essential. One inch of water every week is usually sufficient. If you have a number of trees, consider drip irrigation. These systems are very effective, and many of the best systems are produced in Israel.

Water is especially important for plants grown in pots. One of the signs of water stress is the dropping of unripe fruit. Do not give extra water once the fruit has begun to ripen. This may cause the fruit to split.

Generally, figs will not benefit from fertilizing, which will encourage excessive growth at the expense of fruit. Pot-grown trees need to have their soil changed every two years and their roots pruned.

With the arrival of cooler weather the fig will lose its leaves and become dormant. This is a good time to look at your "naked" tree and decide if any major pruning is needed. Some pruning each year of older branches will encourage new growth.

Pests

Birds like figs. Even fruit that is not quite ripe can sometimes be a target. If you are losing too much fruit, consider putting a net on the tree to prevent the birds from sampling your figs.

Also, try growing varieties with fruit that remains green when ripe. Green fruit is harder for the birds to see.

Gophers can sometimes be a problem. If the gophers in your area have developed a taste for fig roots, try planting young trees in a large wire basket, leaving about 12 inches of the wire above the ground. If they bother large trees, Hava-hart™ traps can be used to trap the animals, which can then be relocated to a nearby field.

Root-knot nematodes are a problem primarily in warmer climates. These are microscopic, soil-inhabiting worms that attack the root system, interfering with normal uptake of water and nutrients. Infestations can continue unnoticed for several years, while the tree gradually loses vigor. The only solution is to obtain nematode-free trees and not to plant in areas infested with nematodes (see Glossary for additional information about nematodes).

Fig Rust is primarily a warm-climate problem. This fungus disease attacks the fig leaves. It first appears as small yellowish-orange spots. Eventually it can cause complete defoliation, but generally does not interfere with fruit production.

Pruning/Training

The condition of the tree you buy will determine the degree of training required to achieve its final shape. If you are planting a young tree that consists of one long branchless trunk, then you will have to start from the beginning of the process for the tree to acquire its final shape. The final shape of the tree should encourage air circulation throughout the tree, let sunlight reach the fruit, and allow for ease of picking the fruit.

At the time of planting cut off the tree to a height of 2 to 3 feet above the ground. During the first growing season the new shoot growth that arises near the point of topping forms the structural branches, or scaffold limbs. During the first dormant season select three or four scaffold branches that are evenly distributed around the trunk. These will serve as the foundation for the tree. Completely remove all other branches. Top the scaffold limbs about 3 feet from the trunk to encourage secondary branching.

Continue to train the trees during the first few years while they are increasing in height and spread. The main objective of pruning is to maintain tree growth in an upward and outward pattern by thinning out interfering branches and removing flat, low-growing limbs.

In warm climates figs need little pruning. This will consist primarily of removing crossed branches and cutting back some old growth to keep the tree vigorous. Leave some growth in the center of the tree to protect the bark from sun scorch.

In cooler climates fig trees are usually trained to grow with three well-spaced trunks. The principle is the same as for warmer climates, but instead of having your scaffold branches begin 2 to 3 feet above ground, they begin at ground level.

Harvesting

Figs will usually yield two to three crops during the growing season. The first crop, called the "breba," ripens from embryonic figs that have remained on the tree from the winter. Northern gardeners may get only a small breba crop, or none at all, as the embryonic figs are usually killed by the cold. In late spring, however, tiny figs will appear at the leaf nodes of the current year's growth and they will continue forming all summer. By late summer or early autumn you should have ripe figs.

Once the figs begin to ripen, check every day or so for fruit ready to pick. Ripe fruit will be soft to the touch and the neck of the fig will be bent under the weight of the fig. In the cooler parts of the country many of the figs that are formed will not ripen because of the short summer.

At some point in late fall you may decide that the weather

is ceasing to cooperate in ripening your figs. To quickly ripen part of your remaining crop, at the close of the fruiting season you can experiment with a method called oleification. This consists of applying one of a variety of oils (mineral, vegetable, olive) to the eye of the fig fruit at a time when it will respond by ripening at a greatly accelerated rate. Using a small cotton swab, dab some oil just on the eye of the fruit. This should be done when the pulp begins to turn pink. Of course, since you can't see the pulp, it's rather difficult to know when to apply the oil. A bit of experimenting will help you get the feel about when the time is right to do this. Applying oil to the figs will usually cause ripening within about a week. Untreated figs at the same stage of development may take as long as 30 days or more to ripen. My personal experience with this method has been mixed. Figs treated this way were not as good as naturally ripened figs. They swelled less and the skin seemed tougher. If applied too early, the treated fruit may drop off.

Winter Care

As mentioned earlier, dormant figs can usually survive temperatures down into the teens, and even below, depending on the age and location of the tree. Young trees are most vulnerable, and cold winds are very damaging.

For those in cool weather areas, there are various ways to overwinter your fig tree. Here's what I do: First prune your tree to one to three trunks and bring the height down to 3 to 5 feet. If leaving two or three main trunks, prune away all branches growing into the center. Try to cut the branches flush with the trunk. (The sap from fig trees can be irritating to some people. If it bothers you, wear protective clothing.) Avoid the temptation to leave many branches, as this will result in an overcrowded tree. After pruning, tie the tree into a bundle and place chicken wire around the trunk to keep out rodents. Pack the space between the wire and the trunk with dry autumn leaves and then wrap tar paper around the outside of the mesh. Place an old bucket on top and your fig tree is ready for the winter.

Alternatively, you can use newspaper, old carpet, bubble wrap—whatever seems most effective and whatever you have lying around the house or yard. Though I have used plastic at times, I've found that encasing the whole tree in plastic encourages mildew to form on the tree. Always leave some way for the tree to breathe.

Unwrap your tree after all danger of frost has passed. Trees that have begun to leaf out are particularly susceptible to frost. If for some reason your tree dies back during the winter, wait patiently. After a while new growth will appear from the roots. You may not get any ripe figs that year, but you can still get an attractive tree 5 feet tall or more.

Another option for gardeners in cool parts of the country is to keep the fig tree in a large pot at least 15 inches in diameter. Leave the tree out in the summer. When the weather becomes cold you can transfer it to a cool spot, preferably between 35 and 50°F, where it can remain dormant until spring. Water the tree every few weeks during the winter so that it will not completely dry out. (If you put it in a heated room during the winter, the resulting growth will be weak and spindly and the tree will not thrive.) Plants grown in pots must be watered regularly during the growing season so they don't dry out. Every other year repot your trees and prune the roots.

Propagation

After you've finished pruning your tree in late fall or early winter, don't throw away the branches lying on the ground around you. From each of these you can create a new tree. Prepare cuttings of about 8 to 10 inches. Don't use the tips of the branches or other very recent growth, as the wood will be too soft. Make one slanted cut just below a node and the upper cut just above a node. If possible, bury them in moist sand or soil, so that only a few inches are above ground. Keep your cuttings in an unheated shed or garage until spring. If you live in a mild climate, you can even plant them in the ground in rows like corn. Space them about 6 inches apart.

With the arrival of warm weather the cuttings will begin to root and the dormant buds will come to life. At this point put each cutting in a separate pot and keep them watered regularly. By early summer you should be able to transplant your new tree to its permanent outdoor location or to a larger pot. The tree should grow 1 to 2 feet during the year but, most important, it will be establishing a strong root system that will enable it to grow vigorously next year.

Another way to obtain beginner trees is to take suckers, which allows you to try out different varieties of trees. Look for other fig growers in your area. Perhaps your town has a garden club. If not, it might have another way for gardeners to communicate. If you live in an area where figs need to be covered in the winter, pay attention as you drive around for wrapped trees in yards. You're sure to find a number of trees that are known for their productivity or for having particularly delicious fruit. Ask the owner if you can have a sucker (or later, when they prune, perhaps a cutting). Frequently, suckers will have rooted. Dig down into the soil a few inches and cut off the sucker below its newly formed roots. This can then be transplanted as a new tree.

These small fig trees make great presents. The perfect time to give them to friends and family is during Sukkot, the festival of the harvest, which almost always occurs during the bearing season of figs. While guests to your *sukkah* are sampling the figs from your tree, you can have ready little pots of new trees to give away. It's also great fun to collect different varieties of fig trees. Other growers will usually be happy to give you cuttings, suckers, or even small rooted trees. If you have a few extra trees, you can reciprocate.

Recipe

The best way to eat figs is fresh from the tree. They can be picked and stored for a short while, but they really don't keep very well. They quickly become wrinkly and mushy. At peak production, however, you may be inundated with fruit. A good solution is to make some preserves.

FIG PRESERVES

1 pound fresh figs
3 cups sugar
3 cups water
½ lemon, sliced crosswise

Wash, peel, and cut the figs into small pieces.

Make a heavy syrup by combining sugar and water in a large kettle and heating slowly over medium heat, stirring until sugar is dissolved. Increase heat to high and bring to a boil; boil 3 to 4 minutes. Add sliced lemon and figs. Cook over medium heat (a good, but gentle boil), stirring occasionally, until clear and translucent, usually about 1 to 1½ hours.

Fill hot, sterilized jars with boiling figs and syrup to within ¼ inch of top. Wipe sealing edge clean and seal.

To protect against mold growth, simmer in hot water bath at 180°F for 10 minutes.

Grapes
(*Vitis vinifera*):
The Vines of Fertility

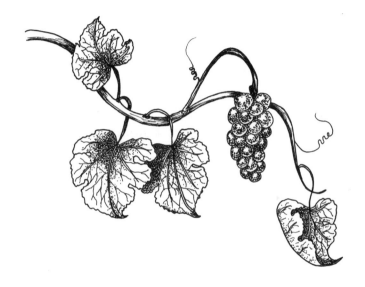

They reached the wadi Eshcol, and there they cut down a branch with a single cluster of grapes—it had to be borne on a carrying frame by two of them—and some pomegranates and figs. That place was named the wadi Eshcol because of the cluster that the Israelites cut down there.

—Numbers 13:23–24

Who can forget the passage in Numbers 13:23 concerning the scouts Moses sends into Canaan? They are instructed to check out the people and the land, and specifically to bring back some examples of fruit. The richness of the land is vividly illustrated when we read how two men carried one cluster of grapes between them. While your grapes probably won't grow quite that large, you can still produce an ample supply of these delicious fruits.

The produce from a vineyard could be enjoyed only after four years of growth. As outlined in Leviticus 19:23–25, during the first three years the fruit was forbidden. During the fourth year the fruit was considered holy and was used for sacred offerings. Only during the fifth year could the grapes be consumed. This shift in status was considered very important in biblical Israel. In fact, a law stipulated that a man could not go to battle before he enjoyed the fruit of his vineyard (Deuteronomy 20:6).

In Isaiah we read verses (5:1–2) that detail the activities associated with planting a vineyard. We read about clearing away the stones, planting the vines, and building a tower among the vines to guard them against animals and people. In *Agriculture in Iron Age Israel,* Oded Borowski suggests that the first task, before clearing away stones, was uprooting the native vegetation. Thus, we have documentation of the entire process entailed in growing grapes: uprooting the native vegetation, clearing the area of stones, planting, hoeing, and pruning.

The grape vine appears a number of times in the psalms, where they bring forth vivid symbolism. In Psalm 128, a wife is compared to a fruitful vine: "Your wife shall be like a fruitful vine within your house; your children, like olive saplings around your table. So shall the man who fears the Lord be blessed."

Rabbi David Kimhi, a thirteenth-century scholar, also compares a wife to a grapevine. In biblical times tender young grapevines were often planted in a hole in the floor of one's home. Later, as the vine grew, it was allowed to trail out of the house into a special garden or vineyard, where it received sun and rain and gave fruit. The rabbi states that the ideal Jewish wife resembles this vine since she, too, is rooted in her home, which is the source of her strength and productivity. The fruit that she bears (i.e., her children) goes out into the world and provides prosperity and blessing for the public.

Psalm 80:9–10, which compares Israel to a grape vine, is especially beautiful:

> *You plucked up a vine from Egypt;*
> *You expelled nations and planted it.*
> *You cleared a place for it;*
> *it took deep root and filled the land.*

Jews frequently resisted foreigners who occupied their land. At Hanukkah time we remember the most famous of these revolts. This one occurred from 168 to 165 B.C.E. and was against Antiochus, the Hellenistic Syrian king. The revolt began in Modiin (halfway between Jerusalem and Tel Aviv in present-day Israel) and was led by the priest Mattathias. It succeeded in establishing Jewish independence.

During the first Jewish war against Rome (66–70 C.E.) a number of coins were struck depicting plants of the country. One particularly inspiring bronze coin from 67 or 68 C.E. shows a grapevine leaf encircled by the inscription, "For the Freedom of Zion."

Another revolt occurred sixty years later (132 C.E.) during the reign of the Roman emperor Hadrian. This time the leader was Shimon Bar Kochba, a descendent of the family of David. An example of the coins from this time period (132–135 C.E.) is shown here in the form of a bronze coin featuring a palm tree on one side, and a bunch of grapes on a vine surrounded by the inscription "Year One of the Freedom of Israel" on the other.

Photo © David Hendin. Reprinted with permission.

Photo © David Hendin. Reprinted with permission.

Grapes and grapevines were also popular synagogue ornamentations. Two of these ornamentations are of particular
beauty: the Bet Alpha synagogue at Kibbutz Hefziba has a mosaic floor dating from the sixth century C.E. that includes a surprisingly lifelike picture of a cluster of grapes. Another restored
synagogue, this one at Kfar Nahum (also known as Capernaum), includes an intricate relief of a grape vine on the wall of
the synagogue. This dates from the third to fifth centuries C.E.

GRAPES IN THE GARDEN

Varieties/Purchasing

There are varieties of grapes suited to almost every climate.
The best way to determine which are best for your area is to
consult your county agricultural agent or local nurseries. Basically, there are three types of grapes.

European or Old World Grapes: These grapes account for the
large majority of commercially grown grapes. They require
mild temperatures. In the United States they are grown in California and, to a lesser extent, in Arizona.

American Grapes: These grapes are native to the northeastern
United States. They are hardy in cold climates.

Muscadine Grapes: These grapes are native to the southeast-
ern United States. They do well in areas of high temperature
and humidity. They are not resistant to cold.

Site/Planting

Grapes need a reasonably fertile, well-drained soil. If the soil is too rich, however, it will encourage unnecessary excess growth. The site should be sunny, and also have good air circulation. A gently sloping hill is the best site, though not all of us have such a location available.

Plants should be placed about 6 to 8 feet apart. Rows should be spaced 6 to 10 feet apart.

Routine Care

Mulch new plants and keep them free of weeds while they are getting established. When you use mulch, wrap or otherwise protect the bottom of the trunk from rodents. (Although mulch keeps down weeds, it is also a comfortable home for small rodents.)

Pests

Many grape ailments, including black rot and mildew, can be eliminated (or greatly reduced) through good air circulation. This is accomplished by choosing the proper site and by pruning.

Birds are a great nuisance to grape growers. The best way to protect the plants is to put a large nylon net over them.

Pruning/Training

To minimize damage to the plant, make sure you put a trellis in place before planting. Use stakes between 5 and 6 inches in diameter and 9 feet long so they can be placed 3 feet deep into the ground. Wires can be run 2½ feet from the ground, and 5 feet from the ground. On the other hand, you can also be creative in your choice of location. Vines can be trained against walls or along fences, or you can build a more elaborate arbor.

Pruning and training grapes are often the most confusing aspects of growing grapes for beginners. There are a variety of methods you can use, depending on a number of factors.

Whichever system you use, remember to prune your vines only when they are completely dormant, usually in January or February.

Pruning has two main functions: to direct the plant's growth and influence the resulting crop, and to open up the plant to allow for better air circulation and exposure to the sun.

Six Steps to Pruning Grapes

1. Select a training system.
2. Remove all dead wood, suckers (shoots rising from the base), and "bull" canes—those more than ¾ inch in diameter.
3. Select canes for "arms" in order to establish the main structure for your training system.
4. Choose canes for spurs. Count the number of buds to be left on spurs and/or canes, based on previous crop load and vigor. The more vigorous the vine, the greater number of buds that should be left on the vine, to increase yield and reduce cane growth.
5. Remove all remaining wood.
6. Cut canes and spurs back to the desired length.

One of the most common ways to train grapes is the four-arm Kniffin system. The fruit is borne on canes (a mature one-year-old shoot) that are renewed each year. This year's crop will be borne on the four long canes that remain on the plant. The two-bud spurs left next to the long canes will provide next year's fruiting canes. Because they are left close to the old canes, they will be as easy to train as this year's canes were. During each dormant season prune the plant back to four canes and four spurs, two to the right and two to the left.

Harvesting

Cut off clusters of ripe grapes with pruners. They should be fully colored and sweet tasting. Many of the varieties have a

delightful fragrance. Once they are picked, grapes will not continue ripening.

Propagation

Sometimes you come across a friend or neighbor who has an especially productive or unique vine that you admire. With the owner's permission you too can have the same variety by making cuttings of the plant. In January or February (before new growth begins) take pencil-sized cuttings, each containing three or four buds. Bury these cuttings three-quarters of the way in the soil in a well-drained area. In areas with cold winters cover the cuttings lightly with straw or leaves to protect against cold winds.

In the spring plant them in rows in the garden or in individual pots. Push the cuttings down into the soil so that only one bud is above the surface. Keep the cuttings well watered and free of weeds. By the following spring you should have well-rooted plants that can go into their permanent location the following spring.

Recipe

My family usually turns most of our grapes into juice to use for *kiddush,* the blessing over sacramental wine, on Friday night. Using juice we have prepared from our very own grapes adds a very special significance to the prayer.

GRAPE JUICE

Making juice from your grapes is very easy.

First, go through the grapes you pick, leaving only firm, ripe fruit. Remove all stems and wash the fruit. Put the fruit in a large bowl and crush the grapes into pulp. Strain this pulp through a cheesecloth, for 6 to 8 hours or more. Let the juice sit overnight in the refrigerator so that the sediment settles to the bottom.

Carefully pour off the clear juice and discard the sediment. You can freeze extra juice. Don't forget to leave room at the top of the container for expansion of the juice while freezing.

Wheat (*Triticum aestivum*): The Most Valued Grain

Moses said to him [pharoah], "As I go out of the city, I shall spread out my hands to the Lord; the thunder will cease and the hail will fall no more, so that you may know that the earth is the Lord's. But I know that you and your courtiers do not yet fear the Lord God." Now the flax and barley were ruined, for the barley was in the ear and the flax was in bud; but the wheat and the emmer were not hurt, for they ripen late.

—Exodus 9:29–32

Wheat ripens nearly two months later than barley, and so was not damaged from the hail that was part of the ten plagues.

Wheat was the most important grain grown in ancient Israel. It eventually overshadowed the importance of barley as a staple primarily because of the better quality of its flour. It was also exported in exchange for other goods. In Ezekiel 27:17, we read: "Judah and the Land of Israel were your merchants; they trafficked with you in wheat."

WHEAT IN THE GARDEN

Even a small garden plot can offer the calming sensation that comes from a large field of this grain. Try to pick a location for your wheat where you can view it from your porch or your living room window. Enjoy the gentle swaying of the seed heads in the wind, and watch as your wheat slowly turns from green to a golden-brown.

Varieties/Purchasing
There are many varieties of wheat. The main difference is between those sown in early spring (spring wheat) and those sown in late fall (winter wheat). Find out from local growers or your county agricultural extension agent which variety does best in your location. In some areas it may be difficult to locate small quantities of wheat for seed. If you can't find seed locally, it is available through a number of mail-order seed catalogs, a selection of which are provided in the appendix.

Site/Planting
Wheat needs full sun. Plant winter wheat in the fall. (I usually plant winter wheat around the time of Rosh Hashanah.) The wheat will germinate quickly and grow quite vigorously. When cold weather arrives, the wheat will become dormant and can

be left outside without any special care. Winter wheat planted too early risks infestation by a pest called the Hessian fly. By fall this pest is usually inactive and there is no risk in planting. Ask your local agent for the best time in your area for planting. It is better to plant a bit late than early. In addition to the risk of Hessian fly infestation, your wheat may grow too much. If the wheat begins to develop a stalk, it will be less resistant to cold winter weather.

In spring, with the warmer weather and longer days, the wheat will begin growing again, and by summer seed heads will have formed. Spring wheat goes through its whole cycle in one growing season.

Routine Care
Wheat needs little routine care. Harvesting will be easier if you keep down weeds within the patch.

Pests
If deer are a problem in your area, consider a bearded variety of wheat. These varieties have an awn (this is like a little spine) attached to each seed covering (which is called "chaff"). It is less attractive to deer due to its prickly nature.

Harvesting
Around the time of Shavuot, when the seed heads have turned light-brown, you can harvest the wheat by cutting off the seed heads. You can then separate the wheat kernels from the chaff (the thin outer covering of the kernel). First, spread a clean sheet of plastic outside so you don't fill your home with floating pieces of chaff. If you have a very small quantity, you can rub the seed head in your hand. For more than just a handful, you will need a flail, which is anything that can be used to hit the seed heads to separate the kernel from the chaff. Place the seed heads on the sheet of plastic and start hitting. I've used a length of curved hose that I hold in

two hands. If you don't have a hose, try a plastic baseball bat or a toy hammer. After you have finished, pour the seed/chaff mixture into a bucket. By repeatedly blowing away the chaff, eventually you will be left with mostly seeds. (It will take some effort to get the seeds entirely free of chaff.) For this separation process you can use a large window fan and pour the seed/chaff mixture in front of it. The chaff will blow away. When the seeds are free of chaff, you can put them through a grinder and turn them into flour. Grain grinders come in three basic styles.

Stone: Stone grinders have two circular grinding stones. One stone turns against another stationary stone. Grooves are cut into the stone radiating out from the center of the stone to the ends. These grooves become shallower as they near the ends of the stone, until they disappear at the outer edges. When grain is ground, it falls through a channel into the center of the two stones. As the stone rotates, it pulls the grain out through the channels where it is ground. The flour falls out the outer edges of the two stones.

In ancient times these stones measured 2 or 3 feet across, weighed hundreds of pounds, and were turned by water wheels or animals. Modern home grinders have stones that are small, usually only about 3 inches in diameter. They're not natural stones like the old grinders, but are made from very hard materials that will last a lifetime if used with care.

Advantages:

- Very durable.

- Adjustable to any setting from cracked wheat to fine flour.

- Much safer if you are grinding grain that has not been completely cleaned of grain-sized stones.

Disadvantages:

- Usually larger, bulky machines that are difficult to store.

- Grind more slowly than impact grinders.

- Stones quickly become coated with an oily residue if you grind oil-bearing seeds or nuts.

Burr: Burr grinders are nearly identical to stone grinders except their grinding wheels are made from steel with small burrs protruding from the sides. These are sometimes called "teeth," and they shear the grain into flour.

Advantage:

- Will grind dry grains as well as oil-bearing seeds.

Disadvantage:

- Will not grind as finely as a stone grinder.

Impact: Impact grinders use rows of "blades" placed in circular rows on metal wheels. One wheel turns and the other wheel is stationary, like the stone grinder. But this is where the similarity ends. The two wheels are aligned so that the rows of blades intermesh and are extremely close, yet never touch the blades on the opposite wheel. The rotating wheel turns at several thousand rpm. As grain is fed into the center of the fixed wheel, the interaction between the two wheels "impacts" the grain and pulverizes it into fine flour as the grain works its way to the outside of the wheels.

Advantages:

- Very small, light, and compact.

- Grinds very quickly.

- Will grind oil-bearing seeds and nuts.

- Grinds grain into very fine flour.

Disadvantages:

- The blades are somewhat fragile and small rocks will damage and misalign the wheels.

- Generally noisy.

- Even on the coarsest setting, it produces relatively fine flour. (You won't be able to crack wheat.)

Propagation

Instead of grinding all your crop into flour, save a number of seeds for planting next season.

Recipe

Making challah using your own wheat flour can be a very special experience for you and your family. A recipe and directions for making challah can be found on page 85.

The following recipe gives a simpler way for using wheat flour that is sure to delight children and help emphasize for them the gift of flour that we receive from God. The recipe is courtesy of the New Jersey Museum of Agriculture.

The process of turning wheat into a popular breakfast food is truly astounding for some children. Let them participate in as much of the process as they can. The younger ones can grind the wheat and mix the ingredients. The older ones can grind and mix, as well as pour the batter onto your griddle and turn the pancakes over as they cook.

WHOLE WHEAT PANCAKES

2 cups whole wheat flour
3 teaspoons baking powder
1 teaspoon salt
2 eggs
2 cups milk
2 tablespoons brown sugar
5 tablespoons oil

Into a large bowl, sift flour, baking powder, and salt. In another large bowl, beat eggs. Stir in milk, sugar, and oil. Add the dry ingredients to the egg mixture and stir quickly, just enough to dampen flour.

Heat griddle over medium-high heat. Grease if necessary. Using ¼-cup measure, ladle batter onto hot griddle and cook until bubbles appear in the center. Using spatula, turn pancakes and cook until golden.

BARLEY (*HORDEUM VULGARE*): THE GREAT SUSTAINER

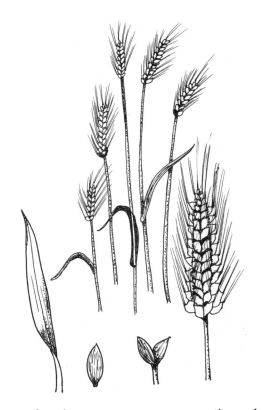

Gideon came there just as one man was narrating a dream to another. "Listen," he was saying, "I had this dream: There was a commotion—a loaf of barley bread was whirling through the Midianite camp. It came to a tent and struck it, and it fell; it turned upside down, and the tent collapsed." To this the other responded, "That can only mean the sword of the Israelite Gideon son of Joash. God is delivering Midian and the entire camp into his hands."

—JUDGES 7:13–14

In biblical times barley was extensively cultivated and barley bread was a staple food. It grows even in poor soil and in areas with low rainfall. In this respect it was valued because it could be cultivated in areas of marginal growing conditions.

In the days of the Judges, farmers in Israel sustained themselves mainly on barley. In fact, according to Leviticus 27:16, barley was so widely grown that the amount of barley seed required to sow a field was used as the standard measure of the field's worth. More than a thousand years later, in Mishnaic times, wheat largely replaced barley as human food, and barley was used mainly as animal fodder.

In the following excerpt from the book of Ruth, we can get an idea about how a barley harvest was conducted. Also, we can read about the important role gleaning had in the Jewish community. It was the landowner's duty to allow the unfortunate in the community to gather grain that had fallen or was missed during reaping.

> Presently Boaz arrived from Bethlehem. He greeted the reapers, "The Lord be with you!" and they responded, "The Lord bless you!" Boaz said to the servant who was in charge of the reapers, "Whose girl is that?" The servant in charge of the reapers replied, "She is a Moabite girl who came back with Naomi from the country of Moab. She said, 'Please let me glean and gather among the sheaves behind the reapers.' She has been on her feet ever since she came this morning. She has rested but little in the hut."
>
> Boaz said to Ruth, "Listen to me, daughter. Don't go to glean in another field. Don't go elsewhere, but stay here close to my girls. Keep your eyes on the field they are reaping, and follow them. I have ordered the men not to molest you. And when you are thirsty, go to the jars and drink some of [the water] that the men have drawn." (Ruth 2:4–9)

BARLEY IN THE GARDEN

Barley is the most adaptable of the grain crops. It grows well in cool, as well as hot, climates. It is even relatively tolerant of saline soils. Though it does not alone have enough gluten for bread making, it does have other uses, primarily in the production of beer.

Varieties/Purchasing
Barley can be divided generally into two distinct types: two row and six row. Each of these has varieties that can be planted in the fall (winter in warm climates) or spring. In addition, you can find varieties that are bearded or beardless. The beards are actually called "awns." They emanate from each seed as a slender bristle about 3 inches long. Bearded varieties are most useful when you want to discourage foraging by animals, especially deer.

Site/Planting
Barley is very adaptable to varying conditions. It does best with a long cool ripening season with moderate moisture, but will also produce admirably in hotter conditions.

Routine Care
Barley, like wheat, needs little routine care during the growing season. Keep weeds down so that the barley will be easier to harvest.

Harvesting
Spring barley ripens in about 60 to 70 days. Winter barley ripens about 60 days after growth begins in the spring.

Propagation
You can save seed from your barley to plant next year. Store in a cool, dry location.

Recipe

The following recipe approximates the barley cakes that were eaten by our ancestors. This recipe can be used as a starting point for a discussion about the kinds of food people ate in ancient times.

BARLEY BREAD CAKES

1 cup barley flour
5 tablespoons sesame oil
2 tablespoons water
¼ teaspoon salt
olive oil
sesame seeds

Preheat oven to 400°F.

Slowly work the sesame oil, water, and salt into the barley flour, kneading constantly for about 5 minutes, or until the dough is smooth and elastic. If necessary, add more oil or water, but dough should be rather oily. On a lightly floured board, roll out dough to ½ inch thickness. Cut out discs with an inverted cup or glass. Alternatively, dough may be pressed into cakes with the fingers.

Place the cakes on an oiled baking sheet. Bake in a preheated oven until lightly brown around the edges, about 35 to 40 minutes.

Lightly brush the tops with oil and sprinkle with sesame seeds.

Yields about five 2-inch diameter cakes.

DATE PALM (*PHOENIX DACTYLIFERA*): SWEET AS HONEY

Deborah, wife of Lappidoth, was a prophetess; she led Israel at that time. She used to sit under the Palm of Deborah, between Ramah and Bethel in the hill country of Ephraim, and the Israelites would come to her for decisions.

—JUDGES 4:4–5

Dates need lots of sun and water to successfully ripen their fruit. They are referred to frequently in the Bible, many times as honey, because of the sweet syrup that was made from them. In Israel today it is difficult to distinguish between wild date trees and those that have appeared through the help of people who casually tossed aside a pit from a date that they had just finished eating.

In biblical times date trees grew in the vicinity of Gaza, which is south of Tel Aviv, and in the Jordan Valley. Jericho was especially noted for its dates. There are numerous references to Jericho being the city of palm trees (see Deuteronomy 34:3 and Judges 1:16, 3:13). In several *kibbutzim* in Israel dates have been reintroduced as an agricultural crop. The popular date-growing areas are the Bet Shean valley and the area around Ein Gedi. Because of this expanding export, Israel has again become renowned for its sweet dates.

In Numbers 33:9 we read about one of the stops the Israelites made on their journey to Israel from Egypt. Their stop at Elim was distinguished not only by fountains of water but by the seventy palm trees that were growing there. By the reference to water, we can assume that the area was rich in ground water—a necessity for palms to grow successfully.

Leviticus 23:40 specifically tells us to use the branches of palm trees in our celebration of Sukkot: "On the first day you shall take the product of hadar trees, branches of palm trees, boughs of leafy trees, and willows of the brook, and you shall rejoice before the Lord your God seven days."

DATES IN THE GARDEN

Of all the plants described in this book, the date palm is the one from which the fewest number of gardeners will be able to enjoy fresh home-grown fruit. First of all, the tree is not suited to small spaces since it often towers up to 100 feet. Secondly, the date palm has very specific climatic requirements in order to successfully produce fruit.

Only the female tree produces fruit, while the male tree produces the pollen. However, since one male tree can pollinate many female trees, commercial growers usually plant only one male tree for every forty to fifty female trees.

Varieties/Purchasing

There are a number of varieties of date trees, but many of them are difficult to acquire. If you live in a date growing vicinity, ask permission from a homeowner or another grower for a sucker from an established female and male tree. You can grow date palms from date seeds; however, you will not know for many years if you have a male or female tree. Only the female tree produces fruit.

Site/Planting

To grow well, set, and ripen fruit, the date needs high temperatures, low humidity, ample ground water, and no rain during the ripening season. Talk about exacting requirements! Place trees 20 to 25 feet apart.

Harvesting

Date palms begin to bear fruit at 3 to 5 years and are fully mature at 12 years. At its peak one tree can produce as much as 150 pounds of fruit annually.

Recipe

Charoset is one of the foods found on the Passover seder plate. In consistency and appearance it resembles the mortar of the bricks that the Israelites used in building during their bondage in Egypt.

Most Jews in the United States prepare *charoset* from a base of apples and nuts. These were the foods that had been available to their families before they emigrated to this country from Eastern Europe. However, you can also make an excellent *charoset* for the holiday using dates. You are more apt to find this type of *charoset* at a seder of Jews from Eastern countries, such as Morocco or Yemen, because they had easy access to these types of foods.

CHAROSET

1 cup dates
½ cup water
¼ cup pecans or walnuts

Cut the dates into small pieces. Combine dates with water and cook in a saucepan on a low flame. Simmer the mixture, stirring occasionally, for 5 to 10 minutes, or until thickened. Add more water if needed. Stir in finely chopped nuts and cook a few more minutes.

Recipe

Raisins and nuts can also be used in the filling for these cookies. They can be added to, or used instead of, the dates.

DATE COOKIES

½ pound dates, pitted
½ pound butter
3 tablespoons sugar
2 cups flour
¼ teaspoon cinnamon
¼ cup water
2 teaspoons orange juice

Place the dates for 2 hours in enough cold water so that they are completely covered. Drain well and pat dry with paper towels. Finely chop the dates and set them aside.

Preheat oven to 350°F.

Cream the butter and sugar together until they are fluffy. Gradually add the flour, cinnamon, water, and orange juice. The dough will be quite soft. Shape the dough into approximately 16 small balls. Make an indentation in each ball with your finger and fill it with ½ teaspoon of the chopped dates. Close the indentation and gently reshape each ball into a circular shape. Place the cookies on a lightly greased baking sheet and bake for 30 to 40 minutes, or until they are lightly browned. Place the cookies on a rack to cool.

POMEGRANATE (*PUNICA GRANATUM*): AS BOUNTIFUL AS THE *MITZVOT*

The opening of the robe, in the middle of it, was like the opening of a coat of mail, with a binding around the opening, so that it would not tear. On the hem of the robe they made pomegranates of blue, purple, and crimson yarns, twisted. They also made bells of pure gold, and attached the bells between the pomegranates, all around the hem of the robe, between the pomegranates; a bell and a pomegranate, a bell and a pomegranate, all around the hem of the robe for officiating in—as the Lord had commanded Moses.

—EXODUS 39:23–26

Though the pomegranate was not as commercially important to the Israelites as most of the other "Seven Species,"
it was held in esteem for the beauty of its flowers and fruit.

The robe of the high priest was decorated with pomegranates, as is noted by the above passage from Exodus. The pomegranate was also an important theme in the decorations of
Solomon's Temple:

> He made the columns so that there were two rows [of pome-
> granates] encircling the top of the one network, to cover the
> capitals that were on the top of the pomegranates; and he
> did the same for [the network on] the second capital. The
> capitals upon the columns of the portico were of lily design,
> four cubits high; so also the capitals upon the two columns
> extended above and next to the bulge that was beside the
> network. There were two hundred pomegranates in rows
> around the top of the second capital. (I Kings 7:18–20)

The shape of the fruit inspired the design of the crowns
that are placed on the two finials of a Torah scroll. These
crowns are called *rimonim,* which is Hebrew for pomegranates.

Pomegranates have also decorated a variety of other things
throughout the ages. Both the synagogues at Kfar Nahum
(third to fifth centuries C.E.), located by the Sea of Galilee and
also known as Capernaum, and the mosaic floor from the synagogue at Bet Alpha (sixth century C.E.), in the Jezreel Valley,
use pomegranates in their decoration. A pomegranate decoration very similar to that of the Bet Alpha synagogue appears
on a coin from the year 67 C.E. Around the picture of the
pomegranate is the inscription, "Jerusalem the Holy."

Because of its many seeds, the pomegranate is associated
with the 613 *mitzvot* that Jews are commanded to fulfill. During Rosh Hashanah, a prayer is said to this effect: "May it be
Your will that our merits be as numerous as [the seeds of] the
pomegranate."

POMEGRANATES IN THE GARDEN

Pomegranates are generally seen as small trees or bushes that grow from 6 to 10 feet or more. They are generally deciduous; that is, they loose their leaves in the winter. In very mild climates they may keep all or most of their leaves throughout the year.

Varieties/Purchasing

Make sure that you get a fruiting variety if you want fruit. Some varieties will just flower. Following are some of the more popular varieties:

Wonderful: The fruit is large and deep purple-red with a glossy appearance. The seeds are small and tender, and the rind is of medium thickness. The fruit matures in late September and October.

Granada: The fruit is smaller than that of Wonderful, but it ripens earlier, about the middle of August.

Nana: A dwarf variety which is good for growing in containers. Plants are usually purchased. If grown by seed, the plants will not necessarily have the same characteristics as the parent plant.

Site/Planting

When fully dormant, pomegranates can withstand temperatures below 20°F. However, they do best in areas of mild winters with hot (even very hot) summers with low humidity. In fact, a long hot summer is important for fruit to ripen. In a humid climate the fruit will not be as good as that from an arid climate. They also need good drainage and relatively rich soil. Place trees 15 to 18 feet apart.

Routine Care

Though pomegranates are drought resistant, occasional deep watering will improve fruiting. Keep suckers cut as they appear.

Pests

Generally, pomegranates are not bothered by serious pests or disease.

Pruning/Training

Prune lightly once a year to encourage new growth. If grown with multiple trunks, let five to six suckers grow into permanent trunks. Trees grown like this seem to fruit sooner and have a better chance of surviving frost damage. Keep in mind that they fruit on new wood. Prune to desired shape.

Harvesting

Pomegranates fruit 2 to 3 years after planting. Harvest when the fruit is red, from late July through September.

Propagation

New trees are usually started from hardwood cuttings. Take cuttings 8 to 10 inches long and ¼ to ½ inch in diameter. You can also dig up rooted suckers or layer low-lying branches. To layer branches, first pick a branch that is long enough to bend down so that part comes into contact with the soil. Place a rock or brick on top of the branch and cover it with soil. Keep the contact point moist, and by the end of the growing season it will have roots. At this point cut the branch from the tree and replant.

Recipe

Think of the surprise when you send someone a small jar of pomegranate jelly as a *mishloah manot* (the sending of food) on Purim. When you make the jelly, save some seeds for adding to fruit salad. It makes an interesting addition.

POMEGRANATE JELLY

4 cups pomegranate juice (about 10 pounds of fruit)
2 to 4 tablespoons lemon juice (depending on the sweetness of the juice)
6 cups sugar
3 ounces liquid pectin

To extract juice, cut crowns off pomegranates and score peel of each in several places. Immerse pomegranates, one at a time, in cool water in a large bowl; break into sections and separate seeds. Skim off floating peel and membrane; discard. Drain seeds.

In a 5- to 6-quart kettle on high heat, combine seeds and ½ cup water. Cover and cook until seeds are soft when pressed, about 10 minutes. Set colander lined with a cheesecloth in a bowl. Pour in seeds and liquid. Tie cloth closed. Wearing rubber gloves, squeeze bag to extract juice. Measure exactly 4 cups. If you are short on juice, add water.

Combine pomegranate juice, lemon juice, and sugar in an 8- to 10-quart kettle. Bring to a boil over medium-high heat. Add liquid pectin and bring to a boil that cannot be stirred down. Boil, stirring, for exactly 1 minute. Pour hot jelly to within ¼ inch of rim of warm, sterilized jars. Wipe rims and seal. Process in simmering water bath for 10 minutes. Let cool on wire racks and label.

Makes seven half-pint containers.

Olive (*Olea europaea*): Provider of Golden Oil

"And what," I asked him [the angel], "are those two olive trees, one on the right and one on the left of the lampstand?" And I further asked him, "What are the two [fruit-laden] tops of the olive trees that feed their gold[en oil] through those two golden tubes?" He asked me, "Don't you know what they are?" And I replied, "No, my lord." Then he explained [what I saw in my vision], "They are the two anointed dignitaries [the high priest and king] who attend the Lord of all the earth."

—Zechariah 4:11–14

In Genesis we first come upon the olive tree in the story of Noah. Noah sends a dove out for the second time to check for dry land: "He waited another seven days, and again sent out the dove from the ark. The dove came back to him toward evening, and there in its bill was a plucked-off olive leaf! Then Noah knew that the waters had decreased on the earth." (Genesis 8:10–11). The olive here symbolizes the renewal of life on earth. Anyone who has ever grown olive trees can attest that they are almost impossible to kill. If you cut them down, they will sprout from the stump, and if you uproot them they will very likely sprout again from a root that has been left in the ground.

This same tendency is incorporated into the symbolism of Psalm 128: "Your children will be like olive saplings around your table." The children referred to here are the shoots that sprout up around the trunk of the tree from the roots. If the main trunk is cut down, the shoots will grow into new trunks and ensure the survival of the tree.

Gideon was a great judge and leader of the Israelites. He was blessed with seventy-one sons. After he died, his son Abimelech massacred all the other sons, but one—Jotham— survived. Jotham then traveled to Nablus, the hometown of Abimelech, where he castigated the townspeople for supporting Abimelech. From atop Mount Gerizim he related to them a parable about giving power to those who are unworthy. In Jotham's parable the trees gather to anoint a king over themselves, and the olive is the first tree asked to reign over the other trees. But according to Judges 9:8–9, "They said to the olive tree, 'Reign over us.' But the olive tree replied, 'Have I, through whom God and men are honored, stopped yielding my rich oil, that I should go and wave above the trees?"

Afterwards, the fig and grape vine were also asked to accept the position. All these trees had much to offer, but nevertheless considered their current task most important. In the end only the lowly bramble, which had nothing to offer anyone, accepted the offer.

In biblical times the olive was not used as a food as we now know it, though it was used somewhat in the same way that we use margarine or butter today for eating with bread. The olive was only used to produce oil.

If you happen to be in Israel after the first rains of winter, you may be able to witness the annual olive harvest, which has remained essentially unchanged throughout the ages. Tarps or blankets are spread under the trees, which are then hit with long poles to dislodge the olives. It is usually the job of the youngsters to gather the fallen olives and place them in a sack for their eventual trip to the olive press. With this technique not all the fruit is gathered from the tree. In ancient times there was always some left for the poor, for orphans, and for widows to gather. As it states in Deuteronomy 24:20, "When you beat down the fruit of your olive trees, do not go over them again; that shall go to the stranger, the orphan, and the widow."

OLIVES IN THE GARDEN

If you live in a warm, dry climate, definitely consider planting olives. Few trees can surpass the beauty of an olive tree. With their silver-green foliage and gnarled trunk, they are excellent specimen trees—individual trees you can put in a place of prominence, especially for their beauty. Do keep in mind that the olives can be messy when they drop from the tree. For ease in cleaning up, don't plant them in an area where the olives will fall and stain a sidewalk or driveway. Also, some people are quite allergic to olive tree pollen.

Varieties/Purchasing

Varieties of olive trees differ primarily in the amount of oil they produce. Therefore, if you primarily want oil as an end-product, pick one based on that criterion. If you prefer to eat the olive, pick a variety that is more suitable for that. A non-fruiting variety is also available if you prefer just to enjoy the tree. Here is a small selection of available varieties.

Frantoio: Small fruit with around 25 percent oil content of excellent quality. Ripens late and adapts to diverse conditions.

Leccino: Small fruit with oil content of around 22 percent. Very resistant to cold weather.

Manzanillo: Medium-sized fruit with oil content of around 20 percent. Does best in mild climates.

Mission: Medium-sized fruit with oil content of around 22 percent. Good quality oil. Very cold resistant.

Sevillano: Large fruit with low oil content. Adapts to diverse conditions.

If you live in an olive-growing area, you can purchase trees at local nurseries or garden centers. Otherwise, trees can be ordered from a variety of mail-order catalogs.

Site/Planting

Olives need a subtropical climate with long hot summers. They can withstand short periods of below-freezing temperature. They need a well-drained soil, but are not particular regarding soil quality. Even rocky soil suits them. In fact, if the soil is too fertile, there is apt to be excessive growth at the expense of fruit production.

Routine Care
Water the trees regularly during dry periods, particularly the first couple of years. Keep suckers pruned back.

Pests
Olives are generally unaffected by any serious pests or disease.

Pruning/Training
Prune newly planted trees by removing the leading shoot at about 5 feet. Then choose three or four strong laterals to provide a basic framework for the tree. Subsequent pruning consists of removing older branches to encourage new growth, as fruits are produced on one year old wood.

Harvesting
Olives will begin fruiting after 3 to 4 years. The yield will increase with time until the tree is about 15 years old. After that it will remain fairly constant. They have a fruiting cycle of one year heavy and one year light. This means that one year you will have a large number of olives, while the next year much less. They need a long hot summer for the fruit to mature. Olives picked green will have a better quality oil, but if left to fully ripen, they will have more oil.

Propagation
You can create more olive trees by rooting stem cuttings. Take cuttings from one-year-old growth that is about one-half inch in diameter. Place in damp sand or other rooting medium, and keep moist but not wet.

Recipe

Every restaurant in Israel that serves Middle Eastern food is sure to bring out an assortment of olives for you to eat with your meal. Once you taste these home-made olives you'll never want to return to the bland store-bought olives that are generally served at home and in restaurants in the United States.

Curing is the process of making olives edible. There are a number of ways to cure olives. In the United States the preferred method seems to be curing with lye. This is the fastest method, but lye is very caustic, and I prefer not to use it. When we lived in Israel, we water-cured part of our olive crop. Here's how we did it:

CURED OLIVES

Use one-pound measures of olives so that you can experiment with different combinations of seasonings. First, the skin of each olive must be cracked, so the water can leach out the bitterness of the fruit. Use a wooden mallet, rolling pin, or whatever else is handy. Place the cracked olives in a quart container and add water to cover. Seal the jar and refrigerate. The water should be replaced every day. Each time the water is replaced you will be removing a little bit more of the bitterness of the olives. After about 3 weeks, sample the olives. They should be only slightly bitter. If you feel that too much bitterness remains, then continue soaking for a few more days.

Next prepare the brine mixture, which is essentially a combination of salt and water. For 1 pound of olives, you will need 2 cups of brine. Bring the 2 cups of water to a boil and stir in 2 tablespoons of pickling salt. Let cool.

Drain the olives and rinse them in cold water. Place the olives in a clean quart jar and cover the olives with the cooled brine. Add your seasonings and keep in the refrigerator about 1 month to develop flavor. They will keep for about 3 months.

ENRICHING YOUR HOLIDAY OBSERVANCE

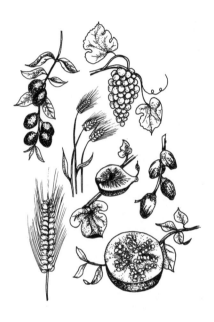

The Jewish holidays are like pearls on a necklace. Each shines with its own brilliance and together, one after the other, they create a remarkable and powerful beauty. This beauty, of course, is not physical but spiritual. As we go from holiday to holiday, we reaffirm our ties to the Jewish people and deepen our faith and understanding of our religion. The holidays give us time to celebrate with our family, each person performing their particular role in the family ritual.

Holidays bring out the best in our Jewish garden. We certainly use and enjoy our garden the entire growing season, but during the holidays we are given the chance to take what we grow and give it added significance.

Tu Bishvat: The New Year for Trees

THE NEW YEAR FOR TREES
BY HOWARD SCHWARTZ

All year
They have kept a careful record
Of everything
The waters of the moon
The slow descent
Of every sun
All year
They have charted the course of every comet
Eyes drawn to the center
To the star that supports
The planet
The beam that holds up every arch
The line that continues into the future
Unbroken
Unchanged.
But tonight
As the light descends into sleep
The trees
All lift their branches to the sky
Cradling the moon

That shines through the night
Like the blossoms of the almond
That have already appeared
To announce
That all fruit that follows
Belongs to the new year
To come.

By the time Tu Bishvat arrives in January or February, the rains in Israel have generally ceased their regular appearance. The soil is saturated with life-giving water, which sets the stage for a renewed season of plant growth. The deciduous trees in Israel begin to "awaken" from their dormancy.

In many cooler climates Tu Bishvat corresponds with the middle of winter. The land at this time is frozen into an impenetrable block. However, though the weather may be bleak and bitterly cold, the days are already noticeably lengthening, and the promise of spring is in our hearts.

This is the perfect time to start planning your Jewish garden. Talk with other family members and decide what you want to grow in the coming year. Send for many of the beautifully illustrated seed catalogs to help you make your decision. There are so many fruits, vegetables, and flowers that you can grow in your garden. Take some time to think about what you want to grow and how you'll use it. If you have lots of room in your garden, you can grow large or sprawling plants, such as corn or gourds. With a smaller garden you may want to confine yourself to herbs or small flowers.

Along with what to grow, you have to figure out how much space you wish to devote to a garden. If you are a beginning gardener, start small. The tidy spot you prepare at the beginning of the growing season can soon become a jungle. Without diligent attention, weeds will sprout up seemingly overnight, and the small, fragile transplants you purchase at the garden center will soon become robust and full-grown.

When deciding on the location of the garden, two things are important to keep in mind:

- The area should receive at least six hours of sun a day. Though some flowers and leafy vegetables will do well with less sun, you'll get the best results from full sun.

- The soil at the site should be well-drained. Go a few hours after a good rain to the site of your garden-to-be. Does the water sit on the surface, or does it quickly soak in? Few plants will tolerate soggy soil. If you can't find a well-drained spot, then consider building a raised bed.

You can make a raised bed two ways. One way is to simply mound up soil 1 to 2 feet high and to a diameter of perhaps 4 to 5 feet. This is most appropriate for a plant such as a fig, which will stand alone. Another alternative, which is more appropriate for vegetables or flowers, is to make a frame from rock or wood. Make the frame about 1 to 1½ feet high, and as large as you wish your garden to be. Fill the frame with soil and you are ready to plant.

In addition to being well-drained, the soil should be rich and crumbly to allow roots to penetrate the soil easily in search of water and nutrients. If your soil is hard, and without much organic matter, consider once again raised beds while you work on improving your soil quality by composting and mulching.

ALMOND (*PRUNUS AMYGDALUS*)

The next day Moses entered the Tent of the Pact, and there the
staff of Aaron of the house of Levi had sprouted: it had
brought forth sprouts, produced blossoms, and borne almonds.
—NUMBERS 17:23

In early spring one of the loveliest sights in the Israeli countryside is the blooming almond tree. Since it usually flowers
around the time of Tu Bishvat, it is associated with this
holiday.

Varieties/Purchasing
There are a number of almond varieties, so check with your
county agricultural extension agent or local nursery about
which will grow best in your area. Plants will generally be available at local nurseries and also through mail-order companies.

Site/Planting
Almonds need full sun and well-drained soil. Though they are
quite hardy, the blossoms that appear early will be damaged by

early spring frost. They also don't do well in areas of high humidity.

Routine Care
Almonds require little routine care, although a mulch of several inches will help keep in moisture.

Pruning/Training
Almonds only need pruning to shape the tree and to remove dead or broken limbs. Keep the inside of the tree open to light and air circulation.

Harvesting
Harvest the nuts from the tree when the shells split. Trees will start bearing after 3 or 4 years.

One of the ways to get you thinking about your Jewish garden is through a Tu Bishvat seder. Over the years this aspect of the holiday has been gaining in popularity. The custom was first started during the sixteenth century by Kabbalists living in Safed in the Galilee.

There are no set rules for a Tu Bishvat seder, only general guidelines. This lets you shape the seder according to your own preferences.

Here's the general idea:

Traditionally, each person at a Tu Bishvat seder drinks four cups of wine, each of which is preceded by the blessing over wine.

בָּרוּךְ אַתָּה יי אֱלֹהֵינוּ מֶלֶךְ
הָעוֹלָם, בּוֹרֵא פְּרִי הַגָּפֶן.

Baruch atah Adonai Eloheinu melech ha-olam, borei p'ri ha-gafen.

Praised are You, Lord our God, Master of the universe, Who creates the fruit of the vine.

After the first cup of wine, we add the following:

בָּרוּךְ אַתָּה יי אֱלֹהֵינוּ מֶלֶךְ
הָעוֹלָם, שֶׁהֶחֱיָנוּ וְקִיְּמָנוּ
וְהִגִּיעָנוּ לַזְּמַן הַזֶּה.

Baruch atah Adonai Eloheinu melech ha-olam, shehecheyanu v'kiy'manu v'higiyanu la-z'man ha-zeh.

Praised are You, Lord our God, Master of the universe, for granting us life, for sustaining us, and for helping us to reach this day.

The first cup is white wine, the second is mixed (more white than red), the third is also mixed (more red than white), and the fourth is entirely red wine. This symbolizes the progression of the seasons, from winter through summer.

It is customary among some Jews to eat five varieties from three different types of fruit. The three groups are:

- Fruits with hard cores, but a soft, edible outside. They are represented by olives, apricots, and dates.

- Fruits with inedible shells or peels, but soft insides. They are represented by pomegranates, almonds, oranges, and walnuts.

- Fruits that are fully edible. They are represented by figs, grapes, and berries.

Some people try to use only fruits and nuts that grow in Israel. If this is not your preference, you may want to eat those fruits from Israel first from among your five varieties.

In between, or along with sampling the fruits, you may want to talk about biblical references to these fruits, or how they might have been used by our ancestors. You can also bring in references or feelings about trees in general, conservation, nature, ecology, or anything else that connects you to this holiday. Some people also compare the types of fruit to the types of worlds described in Kabbalah or to three types of people.

In concluding your seder you may want to consider the following prayer, which is based on the teachings of the eighteenth-century Hasidic master, Rabbi Nachman of Breslov.

> *Master of the Universe*
> *Grant me the ability to be alone;*
> *May it be my custom to go outdoors each day*
> *among the trees and grasses*
> *among all the growing things*
> *and there may I be alone,*
> *and enter into prayer*
> *to talk with the one*
> *that I belong to.*

Recipe

After the Tu Bishvat seder, it is nice to sit down to a meal that incorporates as many of the fruits of Israel as possible. The following recipe for rice uses dates, almonds, and raisins, all of which are grown in Israel.

RICE WITH DATES, ALMONDS, AND RAISINS

2 cups rice
¼ cup margarine or butter
1 cup almonds, blanched and sliced
½ cup raisins
½ cup chopped dates
½ cup water
½ teaspoon salt

Prepare rice, with salt, until it is almost soft. Rinse, drain, and keep warm.

In a large skillet, melt butter over medium heat. Add the almonds and fry, stirring occasionally, until golden. Add the raisins and dates and stir together with the almonds for a few moments. Add about ½ cup water and cook the mixture over low heat 10 to 15 minutes The dates will be soft, and the water will mostly have been absorbed.

Grease a large, heavy pot. Using half the rice, layer it evenly with the almond/date/raisin mixture. Cover with the remaining rice and scatter dots of butter on top. Cover tightly and steam the ingredients over a very low heat for 30 minutes.

Makes approximately eight servings.

PURIM:
THE TIME TO SEND
FOOD TO FRIENDS

Mishloach manot, the "sending of food," is one of the four *mitzvot* associated with Purim. (The other three are listening to the Megillah, which is the story of Esther; giving gifts to the poor; and eating a festive meal.) *Mishloach manot* traditionally calls for sending two kinds of food to at least one friend. One of the foods people typically send is hamantaschen, a fruit- or poppy-filled pastry in the shape of a triangle. If you start planning this year, then next Purim you'll be able to send *mishloach manot* from your garden. This will let you fulfill the *mitzvah,* send a personalized gift to those you care about, and share with others the bounty you have received, through God, from your garden. Following are some ideas to start you on your way.

ZUCCHINI (*CUCURBITA PEPO*)

Varieties/Purchasing
A number of varieties are available in green, yellow, or variegated. Most zucchini grown in home gardens these days have a bushy growth habit. They are readily available at nurseries and garden centers, as are packets of seeds. In books and seed catalogs you will generally find zucchini under the heading of "summer squash."

Site/Planting

Need full sun and relatively rich, well-drained soil. Plant about 2 feet apart. Start indoors 3 to 4 weeks before the last frost date, or sow directly in the garden after the soil has warmed.

Routine Care

Zucchini need little routine care once they are established.

Pests

Zucchini are sometimes bothered by mildew. Affected plants should be removed immediately from the garden. Pick off cucumber beetles and help control squash borer, an insect pest, by lightly covering plants until they start flowering.

Harvesting

For best flavor and texture pick zucchini when they are small. This will also encourage more production.

Recipe

During the peak season zucchini production has a tendency to get out of hand. Instead of begging friends and relatives to take it off your hands, freeze all that excess. Grate the zucchini and put measured amounts in self-sealing plastic bags. When you feel like making some fresh zucchini bread, just take out one of your bags. Thaw the zucchini, drain off the extra liquid, and you're ready to go.

ZUCCHINI NUT BREAD

4 eggs
1½ teaspoons baking soda
2 cups sugar
¾ teaspoon baking powder
1 cup light vegetable oil
3 teaspoons cinnamon
2 cups finely grated (unpared) zucchini
1 cup chopped walnuts
3½ cups unsifted flour
1 cup raisins soaked in water until plump
1 teaspoon salt
1½ teaspoons vanilla extract

Preheat oven to 350°F. Beat eggs, gradually adding sugar, oil, and zucchini. Mix together flour, salt, baking soda, baking powder, and cinnamon. Add dry ingredients to the egg mixture and stir until blended. Stir in walnuts, raisins, and vanilla. Spoon batter into two greased 9x5x2 inch bread pans. Bake in preheated oven approximately 55 minutes.

POPCORN (*ZEA MAYS*)

Varieties/Purchasing
Popcorn comes in a number of varieties. These vary primarily according to the size of the ear and the color of the kernels. Seed is available from most seed catalogs.

Site/Planting
Grow the corn as you would grow sweet corn. (See page 111 for details.)

Harvesting
Make sure kernels are fully mature—hard and glossy—before picking the ears, or they won't pop well. After picking and husking, spread out the ears in a dry, airy place and allow to "cure" for several weeks. Remove dry kernels from the ears and store them in an attractive container.

Propagation
Seed can be saved from non-hybrid varieties.

Recipe

Hamantaschen are the food that many Jews associate with Purim. In Hebrew, hamantaschen are known as *oznei haman*, or "Haman's ears." They recall the story of Esther, the Jewish queen of Persia, and the fate of Haman, who wanted to destroy the Jews.

HAMANTASCHEN

2 eggs
½ cup oil
½ cup sugar
1 teaspoon vanilla
1½ teaspoons baking powder
¼ teaspoon salt
2½–3 cups flour

In a large bowl, mix eggs, oil, sugar, and vanilla. In a separate bowl, sift together flour, salt, and baking powder. Add dry ingredients to liquid ingredients and form into a dough. Roll out the dough on a floured surface to a thickness of about ⅛ inch. Cut out circles using a glass cup dipped each time in flour. Place approximately 1 teaspoon filling in the center of each circle of dough and pinch into a triangle shape. For filling, you can use prepared cherry or prune pie filling.

Make sure the edges are securely sealed and avoid the temptation of putting too much filling into the center of the hamantaschen so they do not burst open. Bake at 350°F. for about 20 minutes, or until golden-brown.

Passover: The Start of Harvesting Grains

Seven days you shall eat unleavened bread, and on the seventh day there shall be a festival of the Lord. Throughout the seven days unleavened bread shall be eaten; no leavened bread shall be found with you, and no leaven shall be found in all your territory. And you shall explain to your child on that day, "It is because of what the Lord did for me when I went free from Egypt."

—Exodus 13:6–8

For many Jews the world over Passover is a joyous family occasion. In preparation we clean our homes and kitchens, taking care that the year's worth of accumulated *chametz*, grains that might have undergone a process of fermentation by combining with water, is discarded. As the holiday approaches we look forward to sitting with family and friends to retell the story of the exodus from Egypt and to thank God for our deliverance from bondage.

When the Israelites were a pastoral people they celebrated an event known as Pesach. It was observed on the full moon of the first month of spring. During this ceremony it was customary for every family or clan to slaughter a lamb or goat at twilight. Once this was done, a bunch of hyssop, a native herb, was dipped in the blood of the slaughtered animal. The blood was sprinkled on the doorpost and lintels of each house. Then, in the middle of the night, the slaughtered animal was eaten, along with unleavened bread and bitter herbs.

In Exodus 12:6–10 a ceremony like this is described. God speaks to Moses and Aaron, and says to them: "All the aggregate community of the Israelites shall slaughter [their lamb] at twilight. They shall take some of the blood and put it on the two doorposts and the lintel of the houses in which they are to eat it. They shall eat the flesh that same night; they shall eat it roasted over the fire, with unleavened bread and with bitter herbs. Do not eat any of it raw, or cooked in any way with water, but roasted—head, legs, and entrails—over the fire. You shall not leave any of it over until morning; if any of it is left until morning, you shall burn it."

Later, when agriculture became more important to the Israelites, an agricultural ceremony was attached to Pesach. This six-day agricultural festival, the Feast of the Unleavened Bread, had originally been a separate spring festival that celebrated the grain harvest. Before the harvest the Israelites would discard all their leavened foods, and eat only unleavened bread.

Eventually these two springtime festivals came to be associated with another event that occurred in the springtime of the year: the exodus from Egypt. Elements of the traditional ceremonies were then explained in terms of the exodus.

Passover celebrates the beginning of the harvest season for grains. In ancient days this was a time of celebration and joy. This harvest season officially began on the second day of Passover, when a thanksgiving offering of a sheaf of barley, the first grain to ripen, was brought to the Temple in Jerusalem. This offering, called an omer, was waved by the high priest at the Temple in gratitude for the produce that God enabled the people to grow from the soil.

As you prepare for the seder, consider that each item on the seder plate has a reason for being there. The items on the plate that apply specifically to the Jewish garden are *maror, chazeret,* and *karpas.*

Maror refers to bitter herbs. The Mishnah (Pesachim 2:6) lists the herbs that can be used as *maror.* Many people use lettuce as their choice of *maror,* though horseradish is also a popular choice at many seder tables.

In Numbers 9:11 we are instructed to eat the paschal lamb with unleavened bread and bitter herbs. This commandment is fulfilled by the *chazeret*. Though it is considered optional, most seder plates include it. The most usual choice for *chazeret* seems to be lettuce, although some people use the green top of a bitter herb, or a second bitter herb, such as a radish.

Karpas can be any vegetable. You can even use a boiled potato. The most common choice is parsley. This is dipped into saltwater at the seder to represent the tears shed during slavery.

You can add a personal touch to the holiday by growing some of the vegetables that you'll be using at the seder table. All the vegetables listed here, except for horseradish, are appropriate for both a cool- and hot-climate garden. In warm climates horseradish should be grown in partial shade. They are all hardy enough so that they will be ready for the holiday in cool climates. In warm climates they will still be in good condition around the time of Passover, which of course comes before the extreme heat of summer.

CHIVES (*ALLIUM SCHOENOPRASUM*)

Chives can be used for *karpas*. In addition to this association they have a spiritual dimension that makes their use at the seder more meaningful. For me chives symbolize the spring renewal that we associate with Passover. The slender green shoots are one of the first signs of life in my garden.

Varieties/Purchasing
Garlic, or Chinese chives, have a mild garlicky taste. They have the same growing requirements as regular chives.

Site/Planting
Chives prefer rich soil and a well-drained location. Though sun is preferable, they can get along in partial shade.

Routine Care

Keep watered and free of weeds. Cut flowers as they form if you don't intend to save their seed.

Pests

Chives have few pests.

Harvest

Cut as needed. The plants produce attractive violet flowers in midsummer. They are edible and are delicious in salads.

Propagation

Chives are usually bought as started plants, though you can also start seeds. If you know someone who grows chives, ask for a division. Simply dig down around the plant and pull out some of the small bulbs with their roots attached. They can easily be replanted. Being perennial, the plants will appear faithfully every year.

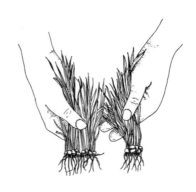

PARSLEY (*PETROSELINUM CRISPUM*)

Parsley, the old standby at the seder table, is beautiful, tasty, and healthy.

Varieties/Purchasing

You have two basic choices regarding parsley: curly or plain. Curly parsley is more commonly used on the seder plate because of its appearance. Its leaves are attractive and its milder taste is especially palatable to children. The other choice is the plain, or Italian, parsley, which has a more pronounced flavor than curly parsley. It is the parsley of choice for cooking. Both types of parsley have the same general growing requirements.

Site/Planting

Does well in sun or partial shade. Most people buy started plants, which should be placed 6 to 8 inches apart. You can also start parsley from seed. Soak the seed before sowing to speed the normally slow germination.

Routine Care

Keep watered and free of weeds.

Pests

Inspect the leaves from time to time for unwanted visitors.

Harvesting

Pick leaves as needed. The root can be used in the preparation of soups.

Propagation

Parsley is biennial: the second growing season you will get some new growth and by midsummer the plant will go to seed. This seed can be used for the next planting.

LETTUCE (*LACTUCA SATIVA*)

There's always room for a few lettuce plants. Try tucking them in among the other, larger plants in your garden instead of in rows. Don't forget to save seed to plant in late summer. This planting will supply you with lettuce into the fall season.

Varieties/Purchasing
There are several distinct types of lettuce.

- Romaine: Long, substantial, well-flavored leaves with loose hearts.
- Butterhead: Smooth, soft leaves, which form a rounded, compact heart.
- Semicos: Relatively short leaves, which are very sweet and crunchy.
- Loose-leaf: Does not form hearts, and may therefore be used for continuous cutting.
- Crisphead (known as the familiar "iceberg lettuce" of the supermarket): Crispy leaves, which form a heart.

Site/Planting
Needs fertile, moisture-retentive soil. It can be grown in partial shade. Lettuce is a cool-weather crop. In areas of mild winters, it can be grown year-round. In hot weather, it tends to bolt. For a continuous supply of lettuce, sow seed every 2 or 3 weeks.

Routine Care
Regular watering and weeding.

Pests
Slugs and snails are the biggest problem for lettuce. They can wipe out an entire planting overnight. You can use commercial slug barriers, or baits, or go out at dusk or dawn and pick them off your plants.

Harvesting
Head lettuce should be picked when mature. Leaf lettuce can be harvested by picking the outer leaves as needed.

Propagation

If you are growing non hybrid-type lettuce, seed can be saved from your plants.

HORSERADISH (*ARMORACIA RUSTICANA*)

Store-bought horseradish can't begin to compare to horserad-ish right from the garden. Add some to mashed potatoes for an extra zing.

Varieties/Purchasing

Horseradish is not usually carried by nurseries, so you'll have to order it by mail or find someone in your area who grows it.

Site/Planting

The plant is quite hardy and it will spread year after year, so put it in a spot where it can easily be controlled. Plants started by root cuttings take two full growing seasons until they can be harvested.

Routine Care

Regular watering and weeding.

Pests

Horseradish is bothered by few pests.

Harvesting

In order to get the best quality root, it is advisable to harvest the plant before it renews its growth in the spring. The root can then be stored in a cool place until Passover.

Propagation

You can easily start new plants by root cuttings. If you have to, you can even plant the roots you find in the supermarket.

Recipe

The nature of gardens is that what begins small generally grows large. At some point during the growing season you may find yourself with more parsley and chives than you can handle. *Tabouleh,* a well-known Middle Eastern salad, is an excellent way to use this excess. We enjoy it just with pita or as a side dish with other foods.

TABOULEH

1 cup bulgar wheat (fine)
1 cup chopped chives, or a mixture of chopped chives and onions
1½ cups finely chopped fresh parsley (preferably Italian type)
½ cup chopped fresh mint, or ¼ cup dry mint, crumbled
½ cup olive oil
⅓ cup lemon juice
3 medium-sized tomatoes, diced
salt and pepper to taste

In a large bowl combine the wheat with enough cold water to cover and soak 10 to 15 minutes. Drain.

Mix the wheat and chives (or onion mixture) and squeeze together so that the juice penetrates into the wheat. Add remaining ingredients and stir to combine.

Makes approximately twelve servings.

Recipe

PREPARED HORSERADISH

horseradish root
white vinegar
salt

When you are ready to prepare the horseradish, first peel and wash the root. Cut into chunks. It is best to chop it in a blender or food processor, as it is very pungent. While machine is running, add white vinegar and continue adding until you have the desired consistency. Add salt to taste.

Recipe

POTATO KUGEL

6 medium potatoes, peeled
1 large onion
2 tablespoons, plus 1 teaspoon oil
2 medium carrots, peeled
2 tablespoons parsley, chopped
2 eggs
3 cloves garlic, chopped or crushed
1 teaspoon salt
½ teaspoon black pepper
1 teaspoon paprika

Preheat oven to 350°F. Heat oil in a skillet and sauté onion over medium heat until golden, about 5 minutes. Finely shred the potatoes and carrots into a large bowl and mix in salt. Pour off excess water. Add onion, parsley, eggs, garlic pepper, and ½ teaspoon paprika. Mix well.

Pour mixture into a greased 9×9 baking dish. Sprinkle top with 1 teaspoon oil and ½ teaspoon paprika. Bake at 350°F. for 40 minutes to 1 hour, or until golden.

Makes 4 to 6 servings.

SHAVUOT: THE LAST GRAIN HARVEST

"You shall count off seven weeks [from the time of the Passover harvest festival]; start to count the seven weeks when the sickle is first put to the standing grain. Then you shall observe the Feast of Weeks for the Lord your God, offering your free will contribution according as the Lord your God has blessed you."

—Deuteronomy 16:9–10

Originally one of the three major pilgrimage festivals to the Temple (the other two are Passover and Sukkot), Shavuot has deep, meaningful agricultural roots. The holiday appears in the Bible under three different names, each of which gives a different indication of its meaning:

> Three times a year you shall hold a festival for Me: You shall observe the Feast of Unleavened Bread—eating unleavened bread for seven days as I have commanded you—at the set time in the month of Abib, for in it you went forth from Egypt; and none shall appear before Me empty-handed; and the Feast of the Harvest, of the first fruits of your work, of what you sow in the field; and the Feast of Ingathering at the end of the year, when you gather in the results of your work from the field. (Exodus 23:14–16)

While Passover commemorates the barley harvest, Shavuot is connected with the wheat harvest, the last grain to ripen. With the grains all harvested, the people could then give thanks to God for the produce they had reaped: "On the day of the first fruits, your Feast of Weeks, when you bring an offering of new grain to the Lord, you shall observe a sacred occasion: you shall not work at your occupations" (Numbers 28:26).

In the *bikurim* ritual the people brought to the Temple their best, unblemished fruits as a thanks-offering to God. Though *bikurim* is no longer practiced, it represents an important moral lesson: the acknowledgement that the accomplishments and success of each person depend on factors beyond our control. In a time when harvests were a real life-and-death issue, Shavuot gave the Jews an opportunity to commemorate the harvest and thank God for the produce from the land.

Shavuot not only marks the end of the grain harvest that began with Passover, but also signifies the culmination of the process of freedom that started with the Exodus at Passover. In post-Temple times, Shavuot came to be associated primarily with the giving of the Ten Commandments on Mount Sinai. Legend has it that the mountain bloomed in anticipation of God's revelation. The lush greenery stood out in stark contrast to the barren desert. We can visualize this inspiring vision when we participate in the Shavuot custom of decorating our home and synagogue with greenery and flowers.

> And from the day on which you bring the sheaf of wave of-fering—the day after the Sabbath—you shall count off seven weeks. They must be complete: you must count until the day after the seventh week—fifty days; then you shall bring an offering of new grain to the Lord. You shall bring from your settlements two loaves of bread as a wave offering; each shall be made of two-tenths of a measure of choice flour, baked after leavening, as first fruits to the Lord. (Leviticus 23:15–17)

Recipe

In the earlier section on wheat and how to grow it, I explained how to grind wheat into flour. (See page 27). Here is another way to make special use of that flour.

In days past, when Shavuot would arrive, every housewife would grind fresh flour from the new grain and bake bread and cakes for the family feast. You, too, can be part of this tradition by adding your own flour to your favorite challah recipe. This recipe calls for 1/2 cup of whole wheat flour. If you use too much wheat flour, the bread will be overly dense. On Shavuot it is customary to bake two loaves of challah. This reminds us of the two tablets of the Ten Commandments. It also represents the fulfillment of the biblical passage in Leviticus 23:17: "You shall bring from your settlements two loaves of bread as a wave offering; each shall be made of two-tenths of a measure of choice flour, baked after leavening, as first fruits to the Lord."

CHALLAH

1½ cups very warm water
4 tablespoons margarine or butter
2 tablespoons honey
1 teaspoon salt
3 eggs
1 package active dry yeast
½ cup wheat flour
5½ to 6 cups white flour

Pour the water into a large mixing bowl. Next, add the margarine or butter to the water and stir until most of it is melted. Add honey and salt. When the water mixture is not hot to the touch, add eggs (reserving 1 egg yolk for later), yeast, and wheat flour. Stir this mixture well, and let stand a few minutes.

Gradually mix in white flour, 1 cup at a time. When the dough begins to hold its shape, turn it out onto a lightly floured board or table and knead about 5 minutes, until smooth. You will probably have to sprinkle flour on the table and/or dough from time to time to prevent sticking. After kneading, place dough in a greased bowl and turn it over, so that both sides are greased. Put a damp dish towel over the bowl and let the dough rise until about double in size (1 to 2 hours).

Punch down the dough by putting your fist on top of the dough and punching downward. Take out the dough and knead a few times to get out all the air bubbles. Return it to the bowl, cover, and let the dough rise once more. If you are rushed for time, this second rising can be eliminated.

When the dough has risen once again and has about doubled, punch it down again and divide in half. Divide each of these halves in three and roll each piece into a long "rope." Using three "ropes" for each loaf, make 2 braids. When you braid the loaves, tuck under the ends of the braids so it looks neater. Put each loaf in a greased 9x5 inch bread pan and let rise about 1 hour, or until almost doubled in size.

After this last rising, mix the reserved egg yolk with 1 tablespoon cold water and lightly coat the loaves. This is easiest to do with a small pastry brush, but you can even use your fingers.

Bake for about 40 minutes at 350°F. When done, the loaves will be light-brown and will sound hollow when tapped on the bottom. Remove the loaves from the oven and place on a cake rack to cool.

Though you don't need much time to prepare the dough, the rising and baking does take time. Because of this some people feel they can't enjoy fresh home-baked bread on Friday night. If you can't begin making your Shabbat challah by 1 p.m. or 2 p.m. of Friday afternoon, consider the following recipe that makes one loaf of excellent challah.

Recipe

CHALLAH (SINGLE LOAF)

1 cup very warm water
3 tablespoons margarine or butter
2 eggs
1 packet dry yeast
1 tablespoon sugar
1 teaspoon salt
approximately 4 cups flour

Prepare your dough as detailed in the previous recipe, though start it on Thursday night. After kneading, place in a bowl. Cover the bowl with plastic wrap and then with a hand towel, and put in the refrigerator overnight.

Friday morning, before work, take out the bowl. Punch down the dough; divide and braid the loaf. Put it in an oiled bread pan and cover once again with plastic wrap and a dish towel. Return to the refrigerator.

When you return from work, take out the pan and let stand outside in a warm place for about 30 minutes so the dough can rise a bit more. Then, bake as above and enjoy.

Recipe

On Shavuot, it is customary to eat dairy foods. A popular, versatile, and easy to prepare dairy treat is blintzes.

CHEESE BLINTZES

3 eggs
1 cup milk
¼ cup water
¾ cup flour
½ teaspoon salt
2 tablespoons margarine or butter

Combine eggs, milk, and water and beat well with a wire whisk. Sift together flour and salt and add gradually to the liquid mixture. Using the whisk, continue mixing the ingredients until they are well blended. Cover and refrigerate the batter for about an hour.

Melt butter in a saucepan and gradually add to the batter while stirring well with the whisk.

Heat a skillet or a 6½- to 7-inch crepe pan over medium-high heat. The pan is hot enough when drops placed on the surface of the pan immediately sizzle. Brush the pan lightly with oil. Remove the pan from the heat, and quickly add 2 tablespoons of batter to the pan. Tilt and swirl the pan until the batter has covered the bottom of the pan. Return pan to the heat and cook until the bottom browns lightly. Using a spatula, loosen the edges of the blintze and invert the pan over a clean dish towel. The cooked side should be facing up. Repeat the process until the batter is finished.

Makes about 12 blintzes.

CHEESE FILLING FOR BLINTZES

12 to 16 ounces dry-curd cottage cheese
1½ tablespoons sugar
1 egg yolk
½ teaspoon vanilla or lemon rind

Strain excess liquid from the cottage cheese and place into a mixing bowl. Add remaining ingredients and mix well. To fill the blintzes, place 2 tablespoons of filling on each blintze, cooked side up. Either roll or fold the blintze to cover the filling, tucking in the sides so it looks like an envelope, or small package.

Melt some butter in a saucepan and sauté the blintzes until golden-brown on both sides.

YOM HA-ATZMA'UT, ISRAEL INDEPENDENCE DAY: REBUILDING THE LAND

*"Land of mine, I have never sung to you nor glorified your
name with heroic deeds / or the spoils of battle / all I have
done is plant a tree / on the silent shores of the Jordan."*
— RACHEL BLUWSTEIN, ISRAELI POET AND PIONEER OF THE
EARLY TWENTIETH CENTURY

If you look at photographs of Israel from the nineteenth and
early twentieth century, you'll notice something unusual: almost no trees. Through literally centuries of neglect, Israel had
been reduced, by the nineteenth century, to a barren, desolate
place. One of the great accomplishments of modern-day Israel
has been to restore the great natural beauty of the country for
all to enjoy. The results have been truly awe-inspiring.

Much of the credit for this transformation goes to the Jewish National Fund (JNF), which was established on December
29, 1901, at the Fifth Zionist Congress in Switzerland. Its funds
were used exclusively for purchasing land in Palestine.

The first tract of land the JNF acquired, in 1905, was Kefar
Hittim in lower Galilee. Other small tracts were added until
the first large settlement area was acquired in 1921 in the
Jezreel valley. This purchase increased the JNF land holdings
from 4,000 acres to almost 15,000 acres.

When purchased, the land in the Jezreel valley was little

more than a desolate swamp. According to the *Encyclopedia Judaica,* after the Crusader period, the Jezreel valley turned into a marshy plain that was inhabited only by nomads. The swamps bred malaria, which made permanent settlement impossible. Nevertheless, the JNF saw the great potential of the area, and in the 1920s the swamps were drained, malaria was eradicated, and settlements were established.

By 1947, just before independence, the JNF had purchased 234,000 acres of land. After independence the JNF shifted its emphasis from land acquisition to land improvement and development. An important aspect of this was planting trees.

One way that we can identify with the State of Israel is by contributing to the growth of its forests and green spaces. You can do this personally when you visit Israel. You can also do it "long distance" to mark Yom Ha-Atzma'ut by having someone else plant a tree in your name in Israel. Granted, you won't know its location or what kind of tree it is, but you'll still be adding to the critical mass of vegetation in Israel and helping to rebuild the homeland of our People.

To have a tree planted in your name (or in someone else's name) you can write, call, or e-mail the Jewish National Fund at:

Jewish National Fund
42 East 69th Street
New York, NY 10021
Telephone: (800) 542-TREE
Their internet address is: http://www.kkl.org.il

This also would be a good time to get involved in the Society for the Protection of Nature in Israel (SPNI). This is a non-profit, non-governmental organization founded in 1953 in response to the draining of the Hulah swamp in the Galilee. Today the organization has close to 100,000 members in Israel and abroad.

SPNI runs nature education programs, organizes local and national campaigns, and maintains a network of twenty-four Field Study Centers throughout Israel. It also organizes a great variety of hikes in Israel.

The address for SPNI's American branch is:

American Society for the Protection of Nature in Israel (ASPNI)
28 Arrandale Avenue
Great Neck, NY 11024
Telephone: (212) 398-6750.
Their internet address is: http://www.spni.org

ROSH HASHANAH: CELEBRATING CREATION

When God began to create the heaven and the earth—the earth being unformed and void, with darkness over the surface of the deep and a wind from God sweeping over the water—God said, "Let there be light," and there was light. God saw that the light was good, and God separated the light from the darkness. God called the light Day, and the darkness God called Night. And there was evening and there was morning, a first day.

—GENESIS 1:1–5

Like any good piece of literature, the first passage of the Bible takes hold of you and draws you in. In succeeding passages we read about the rest of Creation that lasted six full days. On the seventh day God rested. This was the first Sabbath.

Rosh Hashanah is the annual day of celebrating God's wondrous work of creation. Rosh Hashanah is not tied to any national or seasonal event. It is a time of introspection, when we examine our life over the past year and reconcile with those whom we have hurt or offended.

For many Jews who celebrate this holiday with a festive meal, one fruit comes to mind: apples. These are sliced and covered with gobs of honey to symbolize a sweet year. It seems almost too perfect that the holiday usually falls right in the middle of apple harvest time.

APPLES IN THE GARDEN

You don't need much room for certain apple trees. Today you can buy semi-dwarf and even dwarf varieties that produce large quantities of fruit.

Varieties/Purchasing

Apple trees of different varieties offer green, yellow, and red fruit in a range of flavors and textures. Though the majority of apple tree varieties do best in cool regions, some are suitable for warm climates. Local nurseries will carry the varieties most suitable for your area. Mail-order catalogs will expand your choices significantly. Some varieties that do well in warm climates are Anna, Beverly Hills, Dorsett, Ein Shemer, and Granny Smith.

Site/Planting

Apples need full sun and well-drained, reasonably fertile soil. Semi-dwarf varieties can be planted as close as 6 to 8 feet apart.

Routine Care

To get perfect apples you really have to do some spraying. However, you can still get good apples without using poisons. First of all, grow one of the new disease-resistant varieties such as Enterprise, Freedom, Liberty, and Priscilla. In late winter spray the tree with light horticultural oil. This will not harm beneficial insects, but it will suffocate insect eggs and scale.

Harvesting

Dwarf trees will begin to bear two or more years earlier than standard size trees. In many instances the fruit will have to be thinned. This happens when the tree produces too much fruit. In order to allow the tree to develop good-sized fruit, some must be taken off. When the fruits are still small, thin so that there is about one fruit for every 6 to 8 inches of branch.

Propagation

Trees grown from your own apple seeds will usually not produce trees with viable apples. This is because only pollen from a different variety can pollinate most kinds of apples. Therefore, the result will be a hybrid.

Recipe

This cake remains moist a long time. It's a good solution for when you have extra apples from your tree. My family serves it when we have guests for the Rosh Hashanah holiday.

APPLE-RAISIN-NUT CAKE

3 tablespoons margarine or butter
1 teaspoon baking soda
1 cup sugar
½ teaspoon salt
2 eggs
½ teaspoon cinnamon
3 medium apples, peeled, cored, and cut into chunks
½ cup raisins (soaked in water for 15 minutes)
1¼ cups flour
½ cup chopped nuts
1 teaspoon vanilla

Preheat oven to 350°F. In a large bowl, mix together sugar and margarine or butter, then eggs and vanilla. In a separate bowl, mix together flour, baking soda, salt, and cinnamon. Add to the liquid ingredients. Lastly, add apples, nuts, and raisins. Mix all ingredients thoroughly and pour into an 8x8 pan. Double the recipe for a 9x13 pan.

Bake at 350°F for about 1 hour. You will know it is ready when a knife you insert into the cake comes out clean.

SPECIAL HOLIDAY GREETINGS

Before the holiday many of us buy New Year cards, although exchanging cards on Rosh Hashanah is a relatively new phenomenon. In fact, the whole greeting card industry only began in the 1840s with the introduction of inexpensive mail delivery in England, and Hallmark Cards, the giant American company, started operations in 1910. While wishing friends and family a happy New Year, you can also use this opportunity to share your Jewish garden.

Reading through this book, you will come upon a number of uses for flowers. Some can be used as cut flowers, many will stay on the plant so that you can simply gaze upon them. Others you can pick to preserve their beauty. By pressing the flowers in your garden, you can create beautiful personalized New Year cards that will mean so much more to your family and friends who receive them than what you would have purchased in a store.

Pressed flower pictures can be as simple or complex as you wish. You'll need a few simple items to make your project easier and to get the best results.

- A large book that you don't need. This will be your flower press. An old telephone book is an excellent choice.

- A few bricks or other weights to put on the press. You can also use other books.

- Flat-headed tweezers to help in handling the dry flowers.

- Clear acrylic spray.

- A small basket for collecting your plants and flowers.

- Paper suitable for greeting cards.

In the morning, stroll through your garden to find material for your cards. For best results pick your flowers and plant material early while they are still fresh, but after the dew on them has evaporated. Flowers with a single row of petals do best. While you are collecting your flowers, don't overlook other interesting parts of plants. Many flowering, and even non-flowering, plants have beautiful and distinctive leaves. Even many weeds and grasses look lovely when you add them to a dried arrangement. Be open to all kinds of possibilities. Put your treasures in the basket so that they don't get crushed. Don't collect too much at one time. As soon as you have a reasonable amount, go indoors to press everything. Press the flowers as soon after picking as possible. If you wait too long, your plants will wilt.

An old telephone book makes an excellent press. Put the materials inside the book so they don't touch each other, and leave about fifty pages between each group of things to be pressed. When you are finished, place bricks or other weights on top, and set in a dry place. Most flowers take 4 to 6 weeks to dry. Less substantial material, such as thin leaves or grasses, will take substantially less time. Don't open the telephone book during this time or you may wrinkle the flowers.

After your material has dried, carefully pick them up with your tweezers. Place them on a large table so that everything is visible. This will help you see what you are working with when you begin your card.

Now comes the fun part. Let your creative energy flow. You can use one flower or create a small arrangement. It can look lifelike or you can create an abstract design. Place the components of your picture on a blank card. Make sure the paper is heavy enough so that it won't wrinkle later on.

Now you have two choices. If your arrangement is going to be on the inside of the card, you can glue the material in place. Use a glue stick or dilute some Elmer's glue with water and apply with a toothpick or a small cotton swab. If the arrangement is to be on the cover of the card, spray the arrangement with an acrylic spray.

When you send your cards out, you'll be able to share your Jewish garden with those who are close to you. And who knows? Next year, maybe you'll get the same kind of card from them.

Sukkot: Reaping the Final Harvest

Mark, on the fifteenth day of the seventh month, when you have gathered in the yield of your land, you shall observe the festival of the Lord [to last] seven days: a complete rest on the first day, and a complete rest on the eighth day. On the first day you shall take the product of hadar trees, branches of palm trees, boughs of leafy trees, and willows of the brook, and you shall rejoice before the Lord your God seven days. You shall observe it as a festival of the Lord for seven days in the year; you shall observe it in the seventh month as a law for all time, throughout the ages. You shall live in booths seven days; all citizens in Israel shall live in booths, in order that future generations may know that I made the Israelite people live in booths when I brought them out of the land of Egypt, I the Lord your God.

—LEVITICUS 23:39–43

In the Bible Sukkot is referred to as *Hag ha-Asif*—the Holiday of the In-Gathering. This is the time of the final harvest of our produce. By the time Sukkot arrives, most locations in ancient Israel had no doubts or uncertainties about the quality or amount of our harvest. Therefore, we can celebrate Sukkot with a full heart, and thank God for what we have received.

The main *mitzvah* for Sukkot revolves around the *sukkah*. The *sukkah* has two symbolic meanings. First, it represents the dwellings of our ancestors as they lived in the wilderness during their journey to the Promised Land. Secondly, it reminds us of the huts our forebears would erect in the fields during the harvest so they could watch over their produce.

The Bible commands Jews to live in our *sukkah* just as did

our ancestors. Ideally this means eating, drinking, sleeping, and spending leisure time in the *sukkah*. At the very least, traditional Jews try to have their meals in the *sukkah*. Dispensations regarding these *mitzvot* are allowed in cases of rain, illness, or severe discomfort, such as very cold weather.

Hospitality is an important and fun part of Sukkot. Inviting guests into your *sukkah* to share food allows those without a *sukkah* to fulfill the *mitzvah* of eating in a *sukkah*. This hospitality goes back to Abraham, who was well-known for his generosity toward guests.

THE FOUR SPECIES

A *sukkah* is not complete without the Four Species. They are palm, myrtle, willow, and citron. The palm, willow, and myrtle are usually bound together, and are known collectively as *lulav*. This name is taken from the Hebrew word for a palm branch, which is the most prominent of the three bound plants. The "fruit of goodly trees" (Leviticus 23:40) is represented as the citron, which is *etrog* in Hebrew.

There are a number of explanations about these important components of the celebration. I like the following, which is from *Sefer Hahinukh* (The Book of Education), a volume of Jewish religious instruction written in Medieval times. It is attributed to Aaron Halevi of Barcelona, a Spanish Talmudist who lived at the end of the thirteenth century.

> Since the rejoicing [on the holiday of Sukkot] might cause us to forget the fear of God, God has commanded us to hold in our hands at that time certain objects which should remind us that all the joy of our hearts is for God and God's glory. It

was God's will that the reminder be the four species . . . for they are all a delight to behold. In addition, the four species can be compared to four valuable parts of the body. The *etrog* [citron] is like the heart, which is the temple of the intellect, thus alluding that we should serve our Creator with our intellect. The *lulav* is like the spinal cord, which is essential for the body, alluding that we should direct our entire body to God's service. The myrtle is like the eyes, alluding that we should not be led astray after our eyes on a day when our heart rejoices. The willow branch is like lips. We complete our actions through speech, and thus the willow branch alludes to the fact that we should control our mouth and the words that issue from it, fearing God, even at a time of rejoicing. *(Sefer Hahinukh, parashat emor)*

Though some people prefer to purchase the Four Species from Israel, there is no religious obligation to do so. In fact, depending on where you live, you can grow one or more of these plants yourself. Whether you buy or grow them, here is what to look for:

Etrog (Citron): First of all it must have a *pittam,* the thin protuberance at the end of the fruit. It should also have an even yellow color and a basically symmetrical oblong shape. It should not have little black spots on it or any permanent discoloration or disfiguration.

Lulav (Palm branch): It should be fresh and at least 16 inches long. The backbone of the *lulav*—a solid ridge from which the leaves spread—should ideally extend from the bottom all the way to the top. The word *lulav* also refers to a three-sectioned holder, usually made of wicker, that supports a palm branch in the center, two willow branches on the left, and three myrtle branches on the right.

Myrtle: There must be three branches, each at least 10 inches long. Ideally, the leaves of the myrtle should grow in clusters of three at every spot on the stem. Often, however, the three leaves do not emanate from the exact same spot on the stem. You should select myrtle branches that have at least three clusters of three emanating from single spots, preferably near the top.

Willow: There must be two branches, each at least 10 inches long. Preferably, the leaves of the willow should grow in clusters of two at every spot on the stem. Often, however, the two leaves do not emanate from the exact same spot on the stem. You should select willow branches that have at least two clusters of two emanating from single spots, preferably near the top.

BUILDING YOUR *SUKKAH*

According to some traditions, construction of the *sukkah* begins soon after Yom Kippur. A number of kits and designs are available, or you can design your own *sukkah.*

When you enter the *sukkah* on the first night of the holiday, Jews traditionally recite four blessings:

1. Over the wine (or juice):

בָּרוּךְ אַתָּה יי אֱלֹהֵינוּ מֶלֶךְ
הָעוֹלָם, בּוֹרֵא פְּרִי הַגָּפֶן.

Baruch atah Adonai Eloheinu melech ha-olam, borei p'ri ha-gafen.

Praised are You, Lord our God, Master of the universe, Who creates fruit of the vine.

2. Sanctity of the day

בָּרוּךְ אַתָּה יְהֹוָה אֱלֹהֵינוּ מֶלֶךְ הָעוֹלָם
אֲשֶׁר בָּחַר בָּנוּ מִכָּל עַם וְרוֹמְמָנוּ מִכָּל לָשׁוֹן.
וְקִדְּשָׁנוּ בְּמִצְוֹתָיו
וַתִּתֶּן לָנוּ יְהֹוָה אֱלֹהֵינוּ בְּאַהֲבָה
מוֹעֲדִים לְשִׂמְחָה חַגִּים וּזְמַנִּים לְשָׂשׂוֹן
אֶת יוֹם חַג הַסֻּכּוֹת הַזֶּה
זְמַן שִׂמְחָתֵנוּ.
מִקְרָא קֹדֶשׁ זֵכֶר לִיצִיאַת מִצְרַיִם
כִּי בָנוּ בָחַרְתָּ וְאוֹתָנוּ קִדַּשְׁתָּ מִכָּל
הָעַמִּים מוֹעֲדֵי קָדְשְׁךָ בְּשִׂמְחָה וּבְשָׂשׂוֹן הִנְחַלְתָּנוּ
בָּרוּךְ אַתָּה יְהֹוָה מְקַדֵּשׁ יִשְׂרָאֵל וְהַזְּמַנִּים.

Baruch atah Adonai Eloheinu melech ha-olam, asher bahar banu mi-kol am v'rom'manu mi-kol la-shon v'kid-shanu b'mitz-votav va-titen lanu Adonai Eloheinu b'ahava, mo-adim l'simha, hagim uz'manim l'sason, et yom hag ha-sukot ha-zeh, z'man simha-teynu, mikra kodesh, zeyher liy-tzi-at mitz-ra-yim. Ki vanu vaharta v'otanu kidashta mi-kol ha-amim, mo-adey kod-sh'ha b'simha uv-sason hin-hal-tanu. Baruch atah Adonai, m'kadeysh yisrael v'ha-z'manim.

Praised are You, Lord our God, Master of the universe, Who has chosen and distinguished us by sanctifying our lives with God's commandments. Lovingly have You given us this Sukkot, a day for holy assembly and for recalling the Exodus from Egypt. Your faithful word endures forever. Praised are You, Lord, Master of the universe, Who sanctifies the people Israel and the festive seasons.

3. Over the *Sukkah*

בָּרוּךְ אַתָּה יהוה אֱלֹהֵינוּ מֶלֶךְ
הָעוֹלָם אֲשֶׁר קִדְּשָׁנוּ בְּמִצְוֹתָיו וְצִוָּנוּ לֵישֵׁב בַּסֻּכָּה.

*Baruch atah Adonai Eloheinu melech ha-olam, asher kid-shanu
b'mitz, votav, v'tzivanu liyshev ba-sukah.*

Blessed are You, Lord our God, Master of the universe,
Who has made us holy through mitzvot and commanded
us to dwell in the *Sukkah*.

4. *Shehechiyanu*

בָּרוּךְ אַתָּה יי אֱלֹהֵינוּ מֶלֶךְ
הָעוֹלָם, שֶׁהֶחֱיָנוּ וְקִיְּמָנוּ
וְהִגִּיעָנוּ לַזְּמַן הַזֶּה.

*Baruch atah Adonai Eloheinu melech ha-olam, shehecheyanu
v'ki-manu v'higiyanu laz'man ha-zeh.*

Praised are You, Lord our God, Master of the universe,
Who has kept us in life, sustained us and enabled us to
reach this season.

The Walls of the Sukkah

- All materials are appropriate for the walls of a *sukkah,*
  if they can stand up to the weather.

- The *sukkah* must have at least three walls.

- When the *sukkah* is built adjacent to a permanent
  structure, one or more of the walls of that structure
  may be used as part of the *sukkah.*

- The *sukkah* can hold one person or many people, but it must be large enough to fulfill the commandment to dwell in it.

Sechach, *or Roof Covering*

- The *sechach* should be placed after the walls are finished.

- The *sechach* should be made of vegetable matter that was not previously used for anything else.

- It cannot be rooted in the soil, such as the canopy of a tree. Severed tree branches, strips of wood, straw, bamboo, and the like are all suitable.

- Edibles cannot be used.

- It must provide more shade than sunlight, yet the roof materials must not be so thick that they do not let in rain.

- It must be open enough for stars to be seen, but no opening can be more than eleven inches in width or length.

Decorating the Sukkah

One of the outstanding family activities of the year is decorating the *sukkah*. Our family traditionally drives in the first stake of the *sukkah* right after Yom Kippur. We then build and decorate it over the next few days. With a little bit of planning, you can decorate the entire *sukkah* with produce from your garden—just one more way to give thanks for a bountiful harvest.

How you decorate your *sukkah* is dependent on the climate in which you live. In Israel, and other areas with warm climates, palm fronds are a favorite material for decorating the *sukkah*. Those living in more temperate climates will have to create new meanings for plants that were not known in biblical times. Corn, for example, is a Native American plant. We use corn while celebrating Sukkot, and not a plant native to Israel, because that is the material that God has made available to us here in America.

Try stringing different vegetables from the garden. String beans, peppers, or small eggplants will all add interesting shapes and colors to the decorations. Don't use vegetables, such as tomatoes, that contain a large amount of water. They will usually fall off the string after a short time.

Last, don't forget your flower garden. If you can, place pots of flowers around the *sukkah* for additional color. Alternatively, choose some cut flowers and place them in vases along the inside edges of the *sukkah*.

After you are finished with your *sukkah,* stand back and gaze upon it. The bounty that God has given us is right before your eyes.

CORN (*ZEA MAYS*)

We usually put in a corn crop in mid-summer, timed to ripen just before Sukkot. This way we can eat the corn, and the stalks will still be in good shape for the holiday. In my family we put bunches at the corners of the *sukkah* and use it as *sechach,* the roof covering, for our *sukkah.*

Varieties/Purchasing

Three main types of corn can be used in the home garden: sweet corn, popcorn, and Indian corn. Dent, or field corn, is used primarily as livestock feed. The major differences among the varieties of sweet corn are the times they take to ripen. Early-ripening varieties generally have smaller stalks. Try some of the multicolored, or Indian corn, varieties. Corn seeds can be purchased at most garden stores and from seed catalogs.

Site/Planting

Corn needs full sun and rich, well-drained soil. Generous amounts of compost or manure will encourage good growth. Plant seed after the soil has warmed in the spring. If it is too cool, the seeds are prone to rot.

Routine Care

Keep the corn patch free of weeds, especially in the beginning of the season when the plants are still small. Water well during dry periods.

Harvesting

If you are growing Indian corn, leave the ears on until the stalks are dry. Afterwards, pick them and leave in a cool, dry place until thoroughly dry. For the best eating corn, harvest the corn before it is fully ripe. One indicator of ripeness is the condition of the tassels. When they have turned brown, but are still somewhat damp, the corn will be ready to eat. To test, strip one of the leaves partially down the ear and press a fingernail into a kernel. If a milky liquid spurts out, the ear is ripe. Kernels that have no liquid are past their prime. After it is picked, corn immediately begins to convert sugar to starch. For this reason cook your fresh corn as soon as possible.

Propagation

If you are using non-hybrid seed varieties, you can save some of the seed for next year's planting. Non-hybrid varieties are known as open-pollinated corn. In order for the seed to carry the same characteristics the following year, if you plant more than one type, the various varieties must be separated by at least 250 feet. The experts recommend 1,000 feet for absolute purity. (This includes your neighbor's corn patch also.) The distance is important at tasseling time, which is when feathery growths appear on top of the corn stalks.

Corn is wind-pollinated, which means that wind is the

main force involved in spreading the pollen. The pollen is produced by the tassels and received by the silks at the end of
each ear. So, if you have two varieties that tassel at different
times (such as early and late varieties), there is a greater chance
of keeping them pure if you can't manage the distance.

For the most effective protection, completely isolate individual ears of corn. First, decide which ears you wish to save.
Consider such characteristics as size and shape. Before the silk
appears on the ear, cover the whole ear with a water-resistant
bag. When pollen can be seen on the tassels, cut one off. Remove the bag from an ear on a different plant and rub the silk
with the tassel. When this is completed, replace the bag. Do
this with all the ears being saved. The bags can be removed
after the silk turns brown.

Leave the ears on the plant after the other corn has been
harvested for eating. Pick the ears just before you use the stalks
for your *sukkah* and continue drying inside, stripping back the
husks to aid in the drying. Shell the corn on a cold winter
night when you need an interesting family activity and store
in a cool place. Use only the largest best-looking seeds the following spring in your garden.

GOURDS (*CUCURBITA SPECIES*)

Gourds are also great *sukkah* decorations. They are very easy to
grow and come in a wide variety of sizes, shapes, and colors.
Their only disadvantage is that they do take up quite a bit of
room in the garden. If you have a spot where they can spread,
plant a few seeds.

Varieties/Purchasing
There is a vast variety of gourds. They come in all sizes, shapes,
and colors. Many of the seed catalogs sell packets of mixed
small gourds and packets of mixed large gourds.

Site/Planting

Gourds need full sun and do best in fertile soil with good drainage. They can be sown directly into their garden spot, or you can sow seeds a few weeks early. Do not sow seeds more than about three weeks early, as the plants are apt to get pot-bound and growth will be inhibited.

Gourds require a lot of space. Vines can easily grow 20 feet or more. You can allow more space if they are trained on a trellis, but they still will exert their presence in the garden. Space plants at least 4 feet apart if they are being trained on a trellis, more if left to sprawl on the ground. By the way, when gourds are grown on a trellis, the necks tend to be straight. When allowed to develop on the ground, they tend to curve.

Routine Care

Gourds require little routine care. Water regularly until they become established.

Pests

Keep slugs away from young seedlings, either through traps or barriers. Regularly check plants (and particularly on the underside of leaves) for insects. They damage the plant and also spread disease.

Harvesting

The best indication that a gourd is ripe is its firmness. Press gently on the surface of the gourd to check firmness. Browning or drying of the fruit stem can also be an indication. Cut with shears and try to keep at least 2 or 3 inches of stem.

Wash the gourds in warm, mildly soapy water, and then rinse and dry. Lay on several layers of newspaper in a sunny location with good air circulation and let them continue drying for 1 or 2 weeks more.

PEPPERS (*CAPSICUM ANNUUM*)

These days you can buy peppers that are purple or yellow, square, tapered, or round; the variety seems endless. Taste ranges from sweet to dangerously hot. Many of the plants are also quite decorative.

Varieties/Purchasing
Basically, peppers can be divided into whether they are sweet or hot. Most garden centers usually have a variety of pepper plants available. Though they can be started from seed, it is easiest to buy started plants.

Site/Planting
Peppers need full sun and rich, well-drained soil. If starting from seed, sow 6 to 8 weeks before the last frost date. Peppers do not like cool soil, so transplant them after the soil has warmed up in the spring. The ideal growing temperature is 70–75°F during the day and 60–70°F at night. Therefore, in very hot areas peppers are best grown in the fall or winter. Place plants 18 to 24 inches apart.

Routine Care
Mulch and water during dry periods. Keep the area around the plant free of weeds, but be careful of cultivating near the base of the plant, as they have a shallow root system.

Harvesting
Peppers can be picked in the immature stage (when they are usually green) or mature stage (when they are usually red). When picking hot peppers wear light gloves for protection. The oil of the peppers contains capsaicin, an enzyme that is extremely irritating to the mucus membranes.

Numbers 29:35 introduces an additional part of Sukkot: "On the eighth day you shall hold a solemn gathering; you shall not work at your occupations." This day is known as *Shemini Atzeret*. It occurs on the day after the seven days of Sukkot. Some Jews consider it to be an extension of Sukkot. This day marks the demarcation between giving thanks about what was (the harvest from the previous season) and praying for what will be. This is when traditional Jews begin praying for rain and for good crops in the next season. These prayers continue until Passover.

Recipe

Part of the fun of building a *sukkah* is inviting friends and family to share the experience with you. If you plan to invite guests, it's good to have something ready that is easy to prepare and can feed a varying number of people. The following two recipes fit these requirements particularly well. We use these recipes often and grow their main ingredients, basil and lentils, in our garden. Both of these are covered in this book (see pages 144 and 167).

Pesto can be prepared beforehand, and some of it can be frozen for later use. Lentils and rice can also be prepared beforehand and can be eaten hot or cold.

PESTO

2 cups packed fresh basil leaves
3 cloves garlic
¼ to ⅓ cup pine nuts
¾ cup oil
¾ to 1 cup thinly grated Parmesan cheese

In a food processor, finely chop basil. Add garlic and chop. Add the nuts, but process only briefly so that some pieces of nut remain. Transfer to a bowl. Stir in cheese and oil by hand so that it is the consistency of a thick paste. Cover the pesto with a thin layer of olive oil. Store in a container in the refrigerator.

If you have a lot of basil, prepare individual servings and freeze in Ziploc bags. I've found that if you freeze the finished pesto, it is not as good as making it "fresh" from frozen chopped basil.

Recipe

LENTILS AND RICE

2 cups brown lentils
2 medium onions, minced
1 teaspoon cumin
1 teaspoon cilantro, minced
½ teaspoon salt
¼ teaspoon pepper
1 cup rice
2½ cups water

In a large pot, cover lentils with water. Boil lentils about 25 minutes, or until they begin to get soft. Drain and put aside. Fry onions until golden-brown. In a mixing bowl, combine the onions with the lentils, and add cumin, cilantro, salt, and pepper. Mix well and return to pot.

Add uncooked rice to lentil and onion mixture along with extra water. Cook, covered, on low heat for about 20 minutes, or until the rice is cooked. While the rice is cooking, add more water if necessary.

HANUKKAH:
THE LIGHTS OF FREEDOM

*For eight days they celebrated the rededication of the altar.
With great joy they brought burnt offerings and offered fellow-
ship offerings and thank offerings. They decorated the front of
the Temple with gold crowns and shields, rebuilt the gates and
the priests' rooms and put doors on them. Now that the Jews
had removed the shame which the Gentiles had brought, they
held a great celebration. Then Judah, his brothers, and the entire community of Israel decreed that the rededication of the
altar should be celebrated with a festival of joy and gladness
at the same time each year, beginning on the twenty-fifth of
the month of Kislev and lasting for eight days.*
—I MACCABEES 4:56–59

Two activities are central to any Hanukkah celebration:
lighting the menorah and eating fried food. The oil of the
fried food symbolizes the miracle of the oil that occurred on
this holiday. After the army of Antiochus was driven out of
Jerusalem, the Jews reentered the city and cleansed the Temple. According to the account in the Talmud (tractate Shabbat
21b), upon preparing to relight the menorah, they could find
only a single cruse of pure oil that was sealed with the seal of
the high priest. Miraculously, this one day supply of oil lasted
the full eight days until more oil could be prepared.

In Israel doughnuts are the holiday food of choice. In other
countries it is potato pancakes, which are also known as latkes.
Though in most parts of the world Hanukkah is not the most
garden-friendly time of year, your garden can still be an inte-
gral part of both these activities. In cooler climates you can
grow your own potatoes for latkes.

POTATOES (*SOLANUM TUBEROSUM*)

By growing your own potatoes, you can expose yourself to many varieties you would never encounter at the supermarket. Don't plant supermarket potatoes. Seed potatoes you purchase for planting are certified to be free of disease that can harm the growing plant.

Varieties/Purchasing
There is surprising variety in potatoes. They come in blue, red, white, purple, and yellow. They are usually purchased as small seed potatoes, or as "eyes," which are pieces of the potato.

Site/Planting
In regions with short growing seasons, potatoes can be started indoors about 6 weeks before you would normally put them outside. Place the tubers, with the eyes pointed upward, in a shallow tray in a cool, lighted area. They are best planted when the sprouts are ¾ to 1 inch long. Otherwise, plant potatoes outside, 4 inches deep, spaced about 12 inches apart and 2 to 3 feet between rows. If you live in a cool weather area, you can sow the seed potatoes 1 to 4 weeks before the last frost date. In warmer areas sow potatoes as a fall or late winter crop.

Routine Care
When the plants are 8 to 10 inches tall, "hill up" the soil around the stalks to a depth of 5 to 6 inches. This will help prevent tubers near the surface from turning green.

Pests
Potatoes are bothered by a variety of insects and diseases. Two of the most common diseases are potato blight, which thrives in warm, moist conditions, and potato scab, which develops most often during hot, dry summers and when the soil moisture level is low.

Harvesting

New potatoes can begin to be harvested about a week or two after flowering. Poke your hand into the hilled-up soil and gently separate some of the small potatoes from the mother plant. Afterwards, cover the area with soil so the plant can continue to produce additional potatoes.

In the autumn you can harvest full-grown potatoes for storage or for regular kitchen use. After the potato vine has died, let the potatoes remain in the ground for about 2 weeks. This period of time further ripens the tubers and toughens their skin, making it easier to handle the potatoes. Be careful not to bruise or scrape the potatoes during harvest, as this will compromise their storage ability. Store in a cool, dark place.

Recipe

Just as Friday night is associated with the smell of challah baking in the oven, Hanukkah, for many of us, is associated with the smell of latkes or doughnuts frying in oil.

LATKES

6 medium potatoes
1 onion
2 eggs
pinch of baking powder
vegetable oil for frying
salt and pepper to taste

Over a large bowl, grate potatoes and onion. Add eggs, salt, pepper, and baking powder and mix well.

In a large skillet, heat oil over a medium-high heat. Drop rounded tablespoons of potato mixture into pan and fry until edges are crisp and golden-brown.

Using a slotted spatula, turn the latkes and continue to fry them for several additional minutes. Transfer to a paper towel-lined platter to absorb excess oil. Continue with remaining potato mixture, adding more oil as necessary.

Recipe

HANUKKAH DOUGHNUTS *(SUFGANIOT)*

2½ cups flour
¾ cup warm milk (or water)
1 package dry yeast
4 tablespoons sugar
¼ teaspoon salt
1 teaspoon vanilla
1 tablespoon grated lemon rind
½ cup margarine or butter
¼ cup (approximately) apricot or strawberry preserves
vegetable oil (for frying)
confectioners' sugar, for dusting over doughnuts

In a large bowl, dissolve yeast and 2 tablespoons of the sugar in the warm milk or water. Let it sit a few minutes so the yeast can become activated.

Sift the flour, remaining sugar, and salt together into a separate bowl. Add these ingredients to the liquid mixture, along with the lemon rind, softened margarine or butter, and two egg yolks.

Knead the dough into a ball, and continue kneading for 5 more minutes. If the dough is sticky, add small amounts of flour. Put the dough in an oiled bowl and turn over so that both sides are coated with oil. Cover with a small towel and let the dough rise in a warm place at least 1 hour, or until doubled in bulk.

After the dough has risen, roll it out onto a floured board to a thickness of about ¼ inch. Cut the dough with a small round glass or cutter into an even number of rounds. Put about ½ teaspoon preserves on half the rounds. After lightly brushing the edge of the round with water, cover each of these with another round. Seal the edges with your fingers. After all the rounds have been prepared, cover them with a slightly damp cloth and let them rise for about 30 minutes.

Heat oil for frying. Drop the doughnuts into the oil, about 3 minutes on each side, or until golden-brown. Drain on paper towels. When they have cooled slightly, dust with confectioners' sugar.

Makes approximately twelve doughnuts.

OLIVE OIL FOR THE HANUKKAH MENORAH

In warm climates, using oil from your own olive trees to light your Hanukkah menorah can be an exciting and inspiring experience.

In Israel olives are gathered after the first rains of autumn. Sometimes this is done using a long stick to hit the branches and dislodge the olives. The olives then fall onto a blanket or a tarp that has been spread below the tree.

I prefer hand-picking the olives. With this method there is no damage to the tree and you can get every one of the olives. It takes longer, but if you just have a few trees, it won't take that long. Besides, this is a great family activity. Children can strip the olives from the lower branches while the adults concern themselves with the higher branches. Each picker then transfers their olives to a large blanket or plastic sheet. Here, the good olives can be separated from any leaves, twigs, and unsuitable olives.

All the good olives go into a sack and they are brought to a press. The hard part of this may be finding a press that is located near your home. Unlike many other activities, pressing olives does not lend itself to a home activity.

When you get your oil back from the press, you can put part of it aside for Hanukkah presents. Find some attractive jars and fill them with oil. Add a pretty ribbon and a card, and you have yet another personalized gift from your Jewish garden.

ADDING SPICE TO JEWISH LIVING

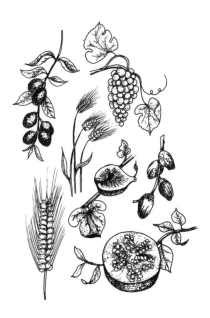

Part of the weekly pattern of our lives as Jews is influenced by the weekly preparation and celebration of the Sabbath. Throughout the week, and especially as Friday arrives, we anticipate the Shabbat, which provides a respite and a break from the rest of the week that has just ended, and a preparation for the week that is about to begin.

In addition, each Jew passes through a number of life-cycle events that are important to ourselves and our family in reaffirming our Jewish ties.

SHABBAT, OR THE SABBATH: OUR WEEKLY BLESSING

*The heaven and the earth were finished, and all their array.
On the seventh day God finished the work which He had been
doing, and he ceased on the seventh day from all the work
which He had done. And God blessed the seventh day and de-
clared it holy, because on it God ceased from all the work of
creation which He had done.*
—GENESIS 2:1–3

When my family and I lived in Israel, the approach of Shabbat was always obvious. Challah was on sale instead of regular bread, the stores were full of people doing their food shopping, and everywhere people were cleaning their homes. There was a general feeling of expectation in the air. In America, unless you live in an area with a large Jewish population, you face a dilemma: Friday night, *erev shabbat,* is usually just another evening after work, and Saturday, the traditional Jewish day of rest, has become the country's major shopping day.

If your children engage in sports or other extracurricular activities, you may find that most of their activities take place on Shabbat. Dealing with these conflicts is sometimes delicate and difficult.

Our family's compromise has been to reinforce the joyous anticipation of Shabbat. We make a great effort to sit together as a family to a festive meal, which is no small matter in suburban America. We light candles, say the blessings, and enjoy an attractive dinner table.

One of the nicest ways to decorate the Shabbat table is with flowers. When you begin poring over the seed catalogs or stopping at the nursery, keep in mind plants that will produce nice cut flowers. Their beauty and fragrance will add greatly to the special feeling we all should have as we sit down as a family on Friday night.

Here are some of the best choices for cut flowers.

COSMOS (*COSMOS BIPINNATUS*)

Cosmos look best in large informal plantings and lend themselves to more informal arrangements.

Besides their beauty they are also a great attraction for butterflies.

Varieties/Purchasing

Cosmos come in a large variety of colors and sizes, ranging from 1 to 5 feet or more. They are commonly available as seeds or started plants.

Site/Planting

Cosmos actually do best in soil that is not very fertile. If the soil is too rich, they will produce more foliage at the expense of flowers. They need well-drained soil. Full sun is best, but light shade is also acceptable. Thin plants to about 12 to 18 inches apart.

Routine Care

Young plants should be pinched back to encourage bushier growth. They may also have to be staked.

Harvesting

Cut new flowers in the morning while they are still fresh.

Propagation

Cosmos will often self-seed. You can also save seed and sow them yourself.

DAHLIAS (*DAHLIAS*)

There is a type of dahlia to meet almost every need, whether it be a compact border plant or a large background in a group planting.

Varieties/Purchasing

Ranging in size from 1 to 5 feet or more, dahlias come in an amazing profusion of colors and forms. They can be grown from seed or "bulbs," which are really root tubers. They are available at most nurseries and garden centers and through mail-order catalogs.

Site/Planting

Dahlias like full sun and moist, well-drained soil. If you live in a cool-climate area, seed can be started 4 to 6 weeks before the last frost date.

Routine Care

Pinch the tops of the larger varieties to encourage bushiness. They may also need to be staked. Remove faded flowers to encourage continuous blooming.

Propagation

After foliage fades at the end of the growing season, dig up the tuberous root clumps and store them in a cool dry place for planting next year.

SUNFLOWERS (*HELIANTHUS ANNUUS*)

In recent years sunflowers have become very popular. If you use them for cut flowers, consider a pollenless variety. If you let some of the flowers go to seed, you will be rewarded with visits by seed-eating birds that would not normally grace your garden area.

Varieties/Purchasing

Sunflowers come in a large range of blossom size, color, and shape, as well as plant size. Sunflowers are usually purchased and grown from seed.

Site/Planting

Sunflowers need full sun and light, well-drained soil. Sow seeds early in the spring. Plants should be thinned to 2 to 3 feet apart so that they will have enough room to grow and develop.

Routine Care

Sunflowers need almost no routine care except perhaps for staking very tall plants.

Harvesting

The seeds of most varieties are not suitable for human consumption because they are too small, but most are excellent for bird seed. Once the flower has faded, cut the flower, leaving a length of stalk. Hang up to dry, and then remove the seeds by rubbing.

ZINNIAS (*ZINNIA ELEGANS*)

Few flowers seem to come in as great a variety of shapes, sizes, and colors as zinnias. They have an important role in almost any kind of flower garden.

Varieties/Purchasing
They can be as small as 6 inches and as tall as 3 feet or more. Blossoms come in various types and in a full range of color. They are available everywhere as started plants and also as seed.

Site/Planting
Zinnias need full sun. While not particularly picky about soil, they do best in fertile, well-drained soil.

Routine Care
Zinnias will branch naturally, but if you prefer your plant bushier, pinch it back to encourage side growth. Cut faded flowers to encourage further flowering.

Propagation
When flowers fade, cut them and set them out to dry in a place where insects will not get to them. At the end of each petal is a seed. Be sure to save just those flowers that are not hybrid, otherwise they will not come back looking like the exact flower that you took them from.

With all flowering plants, once flowers begin to make their appearance, be sure to keep them clipped once they begin to fade. This not only improves the appearance of the garden, but encourages the plants to produce more flowers.

You can even dry flowers to use during the time that fresh flowers are not available. Flowers that lend themselves to drying include strawflower, globe amaranth, statice, and baby's breath. Cut the flowers in the morning after the dew has had a chance to evaporate. Hang bunches of 5 to 10 stems, with the flowers pointed down, in a warm dry place for at least 2 weeks. Afterwards, they will be yours to enjoy all winter and to remind you of the bounty and pleasures of your garden.

Here are some good flowers for drying.

ASTILBE (*ASTILBE* SPECIES)

Astilbe is the answer to areas of light shade where most flowers won't perform to their full potential. The foliage is also very decorative.

Varieties/Purchasing

Depending on variety, you can find plants from 1 to 4 feet tall. They come in white, pink, peach, and red. Though they can be started from seed, astilbe is generally purchased as a rooted plant.

Site/Planting

Prefers moist, well-drained soil enriched with organic matter. In hot, dry climates they need partial shade; in cooler climates, they can tolerate full sun.

Place plants in the garden in early spring or fall, spacing them about 1 to 1½ feet between plants.

Routine Care

Mulch and keep well-watered.

Harvesting

For air drying, harvest just before full bloom. Flower plumes can also be left on the plant to dry.

Propagation

Divide established plants early in the spring before new growth begins.

QUAKING GRASS (*BRIZA MAXIMA*)

The flowers of this ornamental grass produce heart-shaped spikelets on strong stems.

Varieties/Purchasing
Planted as an annual.

Site/Planting
Needs full sun. Does best in soil of average or even poor quality. Sow seeds in early spring.

Routine Care
Requires little routine care.

Harvesting
Harvest when still green, cutting the stems before the seeds have matured. Dry in small bunches by hanging or by standing upright in a warm, dark, and dry location. They look great in arrangements.

Propagation
Plants will self-seed after the patch has been established.

YARROW (*ACHILLEA* SPECIES)

A member of the daisy family, yarrow is a hardy, vigorous perennial. It is good as a fresh cut flower or dried.

Varieties/Purchasing
Yarrow comes in just about all the colors of the rainbow. They are available from garden centers, nurseries, and mail-order catalogs. Though yarrow is available in seed, it is easiest to buy started plants, which are readily available.

Site/Planting
Yarrow needs full sun. The soil should not be overly fertile, otherwise the growth of the foliage will flourish at the expense of the blooms. Soil should be well-drained.

Routine Care

Some taller varieties may need staking. Remove flowers past their prime to encourage new blooms.

Propagation

Yarrow can be propagated by division in spring or in early fall after flowering.

Recipe

On Shabbat it is traditional to prepare a special meal. The following recipe is courtesy of my wife, Nurit, who has figured out measurements for ingredients that she usually uses according to feel. The recipe was handed down to my wife by her mother. It reflects traditional *Bene Israel* cooking. The *Bene Israel* are a group of Jews who have lived in India, according to tradition, for over 2,000 years.

First, you must prepare a paste that is used as a flavoring in a variety of recipes. It is best to prepare a large amount and then freeze small quantities for later use. It will remain fresh in the refrigerator for a couple of weeks.

CILANTRO PASTE

1 pound fresh cilantro
½ pound hot peppers (This is based on the use of a jalapeño pepper. Use less for hotter peppers.)
8 cloves garlic
¾ teaspoon salt

Clean and wash the cilantro, peel the garlic, and cut the stems off the peppers. Put all these ingredients through the fine disk of a food grinder so that it comes out as a puree. Add salt and mix.

Recipe

PEAS WITH RICE

4 cups peas, fresh or frozen
1 to 2 tablespoons oil
2 medium onions, finely chopped
3 medium tomatoes (More tomatoes will make it a bit milder.)
¾ teaspoon salt
¾ teaspoon ginger
¾ teaspoon turmeric
¼ teaspoon chili powder
½ teaspoon paprika
¾ teaspoon garam masala (ground)
1½ tablespoons cilantro paste
2 cups water
1–2 potatoes, peeled and cut up into 1-inch pieces (optional)

In large skillet, heat oil over medium heat. Add onion and cook, stirring occasionally, until golden-brown. Stir the tomatoes into the onions. (The tomatoes should be crushed on a grater, so that just pulp is used. You can also put the tomatoes in the blender. We freeze large quantities of tomato puree during the summer and use it all winter.) Add the spices and cilantro paste. Mix and let simmer for a few moments. Mix in peas so they are covered with spices. Add water so it just covers the peas. Bring to a boil. Cover the pot and simmer, ½ hour, on medium heat. You may add potatoes about 15 minutes before the end of cooking.

Serve with yellow rice (which is rice with just enough turmeric added to give it color).

HAVDALAH: THE BEGINNING OF THE WEEK

Havdalah occurs Saturday evening, and marks the division between the end of Shabbat and the beginning of the other days of the week. For this beautiful and intimate ceremony we use wine, a braided candle, and a spice box filled with fragrant herbs or spices.

The basis for Havdalah derives from the fourth of the ten commandments, which instructs us to sanctify the Sabbath. We do this with oral declarations: Kiddush at the start of the Sabbath and Havdalah at the conclusion.

Originally, sweet-smelling herbs, particularly myrtle, were used in the ceremony. By the twelfth century the use of spices in addition to herbs had begun. It seems only natural that someone would fashion some kind of container for holding them. The earliest known spice box still in existence dates from about 1550. It was made in Friedberg, Germany.

Whatever the plant material, herbs or spices, they have an important task in the Havdalah ceremony. Their rich aroma helps lift up our spirits and refresh our souls in compensation for the end of Shabbat, and the start of the regular work week, with all its attendant preoccupations.

The Jewish garden has a useful part in the Havdalah ceremony. Instead of using regular kitchen spices, such as cinnamon and nutmeg, you can grow plants with aromatic foliage for use in the ceremony. A great variety of plants are prized for their fragrance. Following are some of the more popular ones that are also easy to grow.

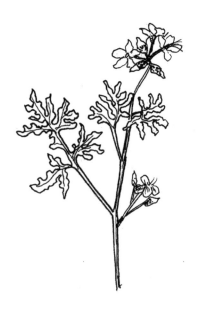

GERANIUM (*PELARGONIUM* SPECIES)

Geraniums make attractive potted plants and have the added bonus of flowers that bloom all summer. Though the flowers are pretty, it is the foliage that is aromatic, not the flowers.

Varieties/Purchasing
Geraniums come in a wide range of fragrances, including rose, mint, citrus, and spice. Fragrant geraniums can usually be purchased at stores that sell potted herbs and occasionally at garden centers with a large stock. Some mail-order nurseries carry extensive selections. (See appendix for a listing of mail-order nurseries.)

Site/Planting
Geraniums do best in full sun with well-drained soil. Though they will tolerate dry conditions, they do best with regular watering.

Routine Care
Geraniums need very little care during the growing season. Removing faded flowers will promote additional flowering. If the plants begin to get too long, cut them back to promote more side growth.

Harvesting
For strongest fragrance, pinch off leaves just before use, and crush slightly.

Propagation
If you know someone with a particularly nice scented geranium, ask for a cutting or two. They root easily. Take a 3 to 4 inch cutting of the desired plant from firm, but not woody, growth. Cut just below a node. Remove the lower leaves and any buds or flowers (leaving just two to three leaves) and place in moist sand or soil. Keep the soil moist, but not soggy. After several weeks, the cutting will begin to root.

BASIL (*OCIMUM BASILICUM*)

There's more to basil than the traditional variety used for pesto. It comes in a range of sizes, colors, and fragrances. It can also do well in a sunny location indoors. Toward the end of summer, transplant some rooted cuttings to a pot, and enjoy the taste and fragrance year-round.

Varieties/Purchasing

Basil can be found in a large assortment of fragrances. Among the more common ones are cinnamon, lemon, orange, clove, and anise. Regular sweet basil, which is commonly used for pesto (see page 117), is available at most locations that sell garden vegetables or from the majority of seed catalogs. Usually you will have to mail-order the other scented varieties of basil, though you will also occasionally see these varieties for sale at garden centers.

Site/Planting

Basil does best in rich, moist, well-drained soil. Though it prefers full sun, it also grows admirably in light shade. Basil is sensitive to cold, and will not do well in cool weather. Unless the soil temperature is at least 50°F, basil will not succeed. Therefore, avoid the temptation to plant outside during cool weather. Sow indoors 4 to 5 weeks before the last frost, or outdoors directly in the garden. The seeds are very easy to grow, and once established, will grow quite vigorously. Thin seedlings to 1 to 2 feet apart, depending on the variety.

Routine Care

Keep the plants pinched back during the growing season to encourage bushy growth. Remove flower buds when they begin to form.

Harvesting

Pick leaves before flower buds appear, when they have the most aromatic oils.

Propagation

Basil can easily be propagated by cuttings or seeds.

MINT (*MENTHA* SPECIES)

With its strong refreshing smell and vigorous growth habit, mint is an excellent aromatic to have in your garden.

Varieties/Purchasing
There are hundreds of varieties of mint from which to chose. Many of these are available only from specialized catalogs.

Site/Planting
Mint does best in rich, moist soil, in light shade or sun. It grows vigorously and spreads rapidly, quickly encroaching on other plants. Keep it in bounds by using a barrier buried partly in the ground, or grow it in a container.

Routine Care
Mint needs little care. Pinch back long growth to encourage side shoots. Remove flowers.

Harvesting
Cut mint in the morning, just after the dew has dried. This is the time when there is the most aromatic oil in the leaves.

Propagation
Mint is so easy to propagate that it almost defies being killed. Just take some cuttings 3 to 4 inches long and stick them in some garden soil. Keep them moist and soon they will root and grow. Better yet, find someone who has mint in their garden: he or she should gladly give you rooted plants.

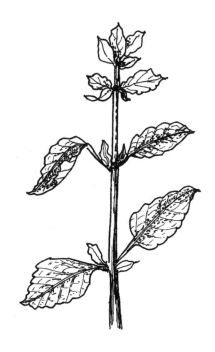

LEMON BALM (*MELISSA OFFICINALIS*)

A hardy, clump-forming perennial with very pleasing lemon scented foliage. Its flowers attract bees and other winged creatures.

Varieties/Purchasing

Lemon balm can be found with green leaves and in a varie-gated form with green and yellow leaves. It is most commonly purchased as a started plant.

Site/Planting

Lemon balm can grow in full sun or light shade. It does best in moist soil. Grow from seed or transplants. Space about 2 feet apart. If you have previously grown lemon balm, you will most probably find it sprouting in scattered spots throughout your garden. These can be transplanted or left to grow in the spot they have chosen.

Routine Care

Needs very little care during the year. Prune away dried flow-ers, and shape foliage to desired size and shape.

Harvesting

Pick leaves in the morning after the dew has dried and before the plant has begun flowering.

Propagation

Mature plants can be divided into a number of new ones. Cut-tings can also be made from stems, or you can start from seed you have saved.

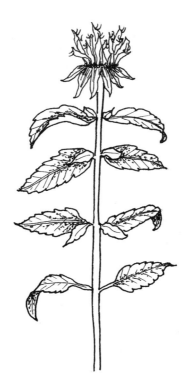

BERGAMOT (*MONARDA DIDYMA*)

This herb is also known as bee balm. (Tea enthusiasts may want to know that this is the herb added to Earl Grey tea to give it its special flavor.) In addition to scented foliage and flowers, this hardy perennial has an added bonus: it has a strong attraction for bees, butterflies, and hummingbirds. So, while you are enjoying the beautiful foliage and flowers, you will also be helping to pollinate your other garden plants.

Varieties/Purchasing
Varieties are available with red, pink, white, or purple flowers. Usually purchased as a started plant.

Site/Planting
Full sun or light shade in hot climates. It does best in moist soil.

Routine Care
Needs little care during the growing season. Keep the plants mulched to help preserve moisture.

Pests
Sometimes bergamot will suffer from mildew. If your plant is so affected, try removing some of the inside stems of the plant to allow for better air circulation.

Harvesting
Leaves are best harvested when flowers form. The open flowers are also edible.

Propagation
Mature plants can be divided, or stem cuttings can be made.

Recipe

On non-Havdalah days, you can use these plants to brew your own herbal teas. Consider adding other plants, such as lemon verbana, which is a tender perennial that can overwinter indoors; catnip, which makes a relaxing tea; or chamomile, which can be easily started from seed. A number of companies sell empty, self-sealing tea bags. (Two of these companies are included in the appendix.) You can also package your own special blends and give them to friends as gifts.

HERBAL TEA

- Pick the leaves as close as possible to the time you intend to use them.
- Use approximately 1 tablespoon of fresh herbs for every 6- to 8-ounce cup.
- Let the herbs steep 6 to 8 minutes before drinking.
- Add honey or sugar or milk as desired.

Experiment with your own combinations, and explore other ways you can use herbs. You might want to use them as a small bouquet on your Shabbat table or as some potpourri to give to friends. You can also press them, dry them, or freeze them.

Planting a Tree to Celebrate the Birth of a Child

When a boy was born, it was the custom to plant a cedar tree; and when a girl was born, a pine tree. When they wed, the tree was cut down and the wedding canopy made from its branches. One day, as the emperor's daughter was passing [through Bethar], the shaft of her litter broke. Her servants cut down a cedar tree and repaired the litter with it. Immediately, the Jews fell upon the servants and beat them up. The Romans went and told the emperor, "The Jews are rebelling against you." And so he marched against them.

—BABYLONIAN TALMUD, GITTIN 57A

These days it's unlikely that you'll find someone so at-tached to a tree that they've planted that they would riot over it. But this ancient, charming custom gives us a refer-ence point that ties us physically to a spot on this earth. We can watch such a tree throughout the seasons and grow to-gether with it.

If you don't think you'll be in the same place until your child gets married, consider planting the tree on the child's bar/bat mitzvah. Instead of cutting down the tree, as was the ancient custom, select several branches that can be used for the *huppah*, the portable canopy under which a Jewish wed-ding ceremony is held. This way, your child can appreciate his or her tree long afterward.

Wouldn't it be nice if our synagogues had extra land

around them? That way we could plant trees there. Even if we moved, we would always be able to return to our tree.

SETTING ASIDE A PORTION FOR THE POOR (PEAH)

When you reap the harvest of your land, you shall not reap all the way to the edges of your field, or gather the gleanings of your harvest. You shall not pick your vineyard bare, or gather the fallen fruit of your vineyard; you shall leave them for the poor and the stranger: I the Lord am your God.

—LEVITICUS 19:9–10

Consideration for the poor and the unfortunate is very important in Judaism. One of the ways the Jewish community helped them was by setting aside the produce from a corner of the field for them. In Hebrew this was called *peah*. *Peah* was considered so important by the sages that they devoted a whole tractate to it in the Mishnah (order Zeraim, tractate Peah). This tractate lists all the specifics regarding the practice: whatever is used as food, is tended, is raised from the soil, is reaped at one time, and is brought in for storage, requires the leaving of *peah*. This includes grain, beans, and peas. Trees such as carob, pomegranate, olive, date palms, and nut trees are all subject to *peah*. Produce that is collected in small quantities at various times, such as berries or figs, is exempt, as is produce that will not keep for any length of time, such as greens.

Since the destruction of the Second Temple in 70 C.E., the agricultural laws have been regarded by some rabbis as binding by rabbinic decree and not by Torah law, and some do not consider them to even be binding in the Land of Israel itself.

While *peah* never applied beyond Israel, nothing prevents Jews who live outside Israel from taking this obligation upon themselves.

During the height of the growing season, many gardeners have experienced the mixed blessing of an overabundant harvest. On the one hand, you are thankful for the produce with which God has blessed your garden. On the other hand, you have to figure out what to do with all those extra fruits and vegetables. This blessing of excess is similar to the allusion I made before to the plight of the backyard zucchini grower wandering between family and friends trying to dispose of zucchini approaching the size of baseball bats.

Why not dedicate a portion of your garden to the needy? Before the harvest is upon you, plan what you will do with this portion you set aside. Once you have done this, you can easily add any extra produce to what you have dedicated originally as your portion set aside for the poor.

Today the poor do not come to our gardens to gather produce we have left for them. In our communities, especially when the needy may be some distance from our home, we need to take our produce to those in need. Most communities have some system for getting food to the poor. It may be through a soup kitchen, a religious organization, or a social service agency. It would be wise to contact the person in charge of such an organization before your produce is ready to ask if there are any restrictions about the type of produce they accept. In some instances there may not be a way to donate fresh produce. In that case you will have to be creative. Perhaps you might consider having your children sell some of your produce door-to-door in your neighborhood (accompanied by a parent, of course). The money can then be donated to a particular charity. This often has the added bonus of involving your children in the process. They can even help you decide which charity should receive the money.

As the garden winds down for the season, you will have accomplished two things. One is that your family will be eating better and healthier from the garden you've tended. The other is that you will have enabled those who are less fortunate than yourself to experience fresh, homegrown produce that you've grown with your own hands.

CITRUS IN YOUR HOME AND GARDEN

In the late nineteenth century, a "new" Jew began returning to the Land of Israel. For these Jews the slogan "to build and be rebuilt" had a very real meaning. The goal was to rebuild what was then Palestine in preparation for a new Jewish state. At the same time they were rebuilding themselves: transforming themselves into a new type of Jew that had long vanished from the scene—self-sufficient, proud, and intimately tied to the land and the soil.

Even before the creation of the new state and then on into its early years, one crop became clearly representative of Israel: citrus. Jewish involvement in citrus started in 1855, when Sir Moses Montefiore made the first Jewish land purchase in Palestine—twenty-five acres of orange groves in Jaffa.

A special experience awaits anyone who has traveled through Israel's central region when the citrus flowers open to spread their intoxicating fragrance throughout the countryside. During the last few years, however, the acreage in citrus in the center of Israel has steadily declined as development has put increasing demands on the land. From 1980 to 1990, citrus production declined from about 4,300 hectares to about 2,500 hectares. However, at the same time, there has been a push toward planting citrus groves in the central Negev, particularly in the area around Kibbutzim Zeelim and Urim. Since 1990, 95 percent of the new citrus plantings have been in this area. If this continues, maybe in a few years we'll be able to travel in the Negev and experience the same heady fragrance that we once associated further north with the Sharon Plain.

You can bring the fragrance of citrus to your Jewish garden. When your tree blooms, close your eyes and you'll be able to imagine yourself driving down Israel's coastal highway with the windows down to catch the fragrant breeze.

Varieties/Purchasing

There are many varieties of citrus.

Lemons (Citrus limon)

Lisbon: A vigorous, relatively cold-resistant tree. Most of the fruit ripens in the fall and early winter, but some remains on the tree all year.

Meyer: Smaller and more cold-resistant than the Lisbon. The fruit has a mild flavor and a high juice content. It will produce well in a pot. Our Meyer lemon supplies us with a steady supply of lemons for kitchen use.

Oranges (Citrus sinensis)

Jaffa: Largest of the sweet oranges.

Shamouti: Fragrant sweet fruit with few seeds. Tree is upright with large leaves.

Valencia: Fruit matures later than that of Washington, usually from April to June. Planting both varieties assures you of a year-round supply of fruit.

Washington Navel: Produces large fruit that can stay on the tree for 3 to 4 months. Fruit matures usually from mid-November to February.

Tangerine (Citrus reticulata)

Satsuma Mandarin: One of the best citrus choices for cooler areas. It will survive down to 18°F. with only slight damage. The large fruit ripens very early in the season. The tree itself is small and thornless.

If you live in a citrus-growing area, you will find trees at your local nursery. Those living in cooler climates have easy access through mail-order catalogs.

Site/Planting
Citrus needs a warm climate. They do best in well-drained, light, and relatively fertile soil.

Routine Care
Citrus trees are not usually mulched. However, the area around the trunk should be kept free of weeds and grass that will compete with the feeder roots of the tree. Deep, infrequent watering is best for citrus—they don't do well in soil that is constantly wet. Young trees need to be watered more frequently until they are established.

Citrus can adapt themselves as indoor plants in areas with

cold winters. Find your tree a location with as much sun as possible. To prevent the air from being too arid, place a water-filled tray with pebbles beneath the tree so the water can evaporate and keep the immediate area humid. Bring the tree outdoors in the summer and indoors before the temperatures dip much below 50°F. Make sure that all changes of location are gradual. Good varieties for indoor growing are: Otaheite orange, Meyer lemon, and Calamondin orange.

Pruning/Training
Prune the tree to keep fruit within reach of easy picking.

Harvesting
Depending on the variety, fruit can remain on the tree for several weeks to several months.

Propagation
Though you can grow seeds from fruit you buy at the store, if you want to grow your tree for fruit it is best to purchase a tree from a grower.

A BIBLE GARDEN FOR YOU AND YOUR CHILDREN

For many of our children, the Bible is a distant, somewhat abstract text. They hear the Torah read in Temple. If they attend Hebrew School, they will probably learn some Bible stories. Generally, however, it has little impact on their lives. Competing as it does with schoolwork, TV, Nintendo, and other leisure-time activities, the Bible is given little time and thought.

You can, however, make the Bible literally come alive for your children by planting a Bible garden. This can be done wherever you live. A possible starting point is with *shivat haminim,* the seven varieties of plants that were discussed in the beginning of the book. In addition to these, many other plants can be grown. Some are as common as the willow and everyday garlic; others will challenge your gardening skills.

You can obtain a list of Bible plants from a number of sources. The *Encyclopedia Judaica* has an extensive listing under the heading "Plants." Some Bible concordances also list plants separately in a subject index, and a number of books have been published about plants in the Bible.

There are also ways to obtain information about Bible gardens on-line.

- Neot Kedumim. A 625-acre biblical landscape reserve in Israel. It is located in the Modiin region, halfway between Jerusalem and Tel Aviv. http://www.neot-kedumim.org.il.

- Warsaw Biblical Gardens. One hundred and ten species of plants on just under an acre of land in Warsaw, Indiana. http://www.warsawbiblicalgardens. org/index.html.

Once you have a list, a Bible concordance will give you the relevant passage(s) where it appears in the Bible. Read these over as a family to see which ones particularly interest you. With your children, draw connections between the plant as they see it today and how it was used thousands of years ago.

If you want to get fancy, write little weather-proof placards to put next to each plant, with a favorite Biblical passage relating to it. Encourage your synagogue to set aside a small garden plot for a Bible garden. This would be a great project for a Hebrew School, and during the summer several schoolchildren can earn pocket money by tending it.

There are a whole host of other plants that can be added to a Bible garden. Following is a selection, although seeds or plants of some might be difficult to find.

ACACIA (*ACACIA RADDIANA*)

And let them make Me a sanctuary that I may dwell among them. Exactly as I show you—the pattern of the Tabernacle and the pattern of all its furnishings—so shall you make it. They shall make an ark of acacia wood, two and a half cubits long, a cubit and a half wide, and a cubit and a half high.
—Exodus 25:8–10

The acacia attains a height of 15 to 25 feet. The fruit is a many-seeded pod that is a valuable food for desert animals.

CAROB (*CERATONIA SILIQUA*)

Carob trees certainly grew in Israel during the time of our ancestors, and they continue to grace Israel's landscape today. For that reason I have decided to include them.

Carobs are multi-stemmed trees with glossy, evergreen leaves and a broad, spreading form. They do best in areas where the temperature does not fall below freezing, and also is not excessively high.

To ensure a good crop, both female (pod-producing) and male (pollen-producing) trees should be planted. The ground seed pods are the source of carob powder, a chocolate substitute.

FLAX (*LINUM USITATISSIMUM*)

So they bound him with two new ropes and brought him [Samson] up from the rock. When he reached Lehi, the Philistines came shouting to meet him. Thereupon the spirit of the Lord gripped him, and the ropes on his arms became like flax that catches fire; the bonds melted off his hands.

—JUDGES 15:13–14

In ancient times flax was harvested whole and left to dry. The stalks were then steeped in water until the outer part partially decayed. Next, the stalks were split and combed until the useful threads separated and peeled off from the stalk. The short, fine threads were then woven into linen.

HYSSOP, SYRIAN (*ORIGANUM SYRIACUM*)

Moses then summoned all the elders of Israel and said to them, "Go, pick out lambs for your families, and slaughter the Passover offering. Take a bunch of hyssop, dip it in the blood that is in the basin and apply some of the blood that is in the basin to the lintel and to the two doorposts. None of you shall go outside the door of his house until morning. For when the Lord goes through to smite the Egyptians, He will see the blood on the lintel and the two doorposts, and the Lord will pass

over the door and not let the Destroyer enter and smite your
home.

—Exodus 12:21–23

Hyssop is a stout, many-stemmed hairy gray shrub native to the Middle East. It can grow to be 2 feet tall.

LENTILS (*LENS ESCULENTA*)

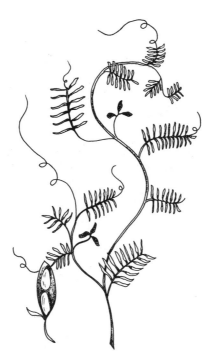

Once when Jacob was cooking a stew, Esau came in from the
open, famished. And Esau said to Jacob, "Give me some of
that red stuff to gulp down, for I am famished"—which is why
he was named Edom. Jacob said, "First sell me your
birthright." And Esau said, "I am at the point of death, so of
what use is my birthright to me?" But Jacob said, "Swear to
me first." So he swore to him, and sold his birthright to Jacob.
Jacob then gave Esau bread and lentil stew; he ate and drank,
and he rose and went away. Thus did Esau spurn the
birthright.

—Genesis 25:29–34

The lentil is a bushy, semi-viney annual growing 12 to 18 inches in height. It has numerous soft, hairy branches, and many flowers. It does best in dry climates.

MYRTLE (*MYRTUS COMMUNIS*)

They found written in the Teaching that the Lord had commanded Moses that the Israelites must dwell in booths during the festival of the seventh month, and that they must announce and proclaim throughout all their towns and Jerusalem as follows, "Go out to the mountains and bring leafy branches of olive trees, pine trees, myrtles, palms and [other] leafy trees to make booths, as it is written."

—NEHEMIAH 8:14–15

Myrtle is usually grown as a shrub, but it can also be trained as a small tree. It is prized for its attractive and aromatic foliage. It needs full sun.

SYCAMORE (*FICUS SYCOMORUS*)

Amos answered Amaziah: "I am not a prophet, and I am not a prophet's disciple. I am a cattle breeder and a tender of sycamore figs."

—Amos 7:14

The sycamore produces up to six crops a year, mostly during the summer months. Although used as food, they were considered inferior to the fig. In the time of David and Solomon they were used extensively in building (I Chronicles 27:28).

TEREBINTH, ATLANTIC (*PISTACIA ATLANTICA*); TEREBINTH, PALESTINE (*PISTACIA PALAESTINA*)

Absalom encountered some of David's followers. Absalom was riding on a mule, and as the mule passed under the tangled branches of a great terebinth, his hair got caught in the terebinth; he was held between heaven and earth as the mule under him kept going.

—II Samuel 18:9

Both the Atlantic and Palestine terebinth are native to Israel. The Palestine terebinth is the one in which David's son, Absalom, caught his hair when fleeing from the field of Ephraim and in which he met his death. In areas where they have been left alone, such as remote desert areas, they can reach many hundred of years in age and grow to be large, impressive-looking trees.

CONCLUSION

This book is meant as a jumping-off point for the reader. Its real value begins when you start to make your own personal connections between your garden and your religious observance.

In preparing food from your garden, you are bound only by your imagination. You can make foods "Jewish" as you use them to strengthen your appreciation, enjoyment, or understanding of the holidays and rituals of Judaism. A plant becomes part of your Jewish garden for the same reasons.

Our close connection to plants and the natural world around us did not end in biblical days. As Jews moved into new countries that had different climates from Israel's, they assigned new meanings to the plants around them. We can do the same today wherever we may be living. This can open us to the possibilities of our faith and of the world around us, even as we remember the bounty of the Land of Israel, both in biblical times and today.

GLOSSARY

Annual   A plant whose entire life cycle is completed in a single growing season.

Bar/Bat Mitzvah   A child who has reached the age of thirteen and is expected to accept adult religious responsibilities.

Bolt   Premature flowering of a plant at the expense of the vegetative development. The resulting vegetable usually becomes bitter as a result of bolting.

Bud   The growing point or protrusion on a stem where a leaf, shoot, or flower appears.

Cane   A hollow or pithy jointed stem, especially on grapes or raspberries.

Challah   The braided bread traditionally prepared by Jews for the Sabbath.

Charoset   One of the symbolic foods of the Passover seder. Its color and consistency remind us of the bricks and mortar used by the Israelite slaves in Egypt.

Cheesecloth   A loosely woven cotton gauze, used in cooking for straining.

Chilling requirement   The need of certain plants to have a specific period of dormancy below a particular temperature for flowering or fruiting to begin.

Compost   Soil-improving and nutrient-rich material resulting from decomposition of organic materials.

Cutting   A section of a plant that can be cut off and grown into a new plant.

Deciduous Trees or shrubs that drop their leaves at the end of the growing season and remain leafless and dormant during the winter.

Dormant When a plant is inactive. It is capable of growth once conditions become favorable.

Dwarf A plant smaller at maturity than others of the same species.

Germination Sprouting of a seed and beginning of active growth.

Gluten A component of wheat flour that is important in the bread-making process.

Hamantaschen The three-cornered pastry that is eaten during Purim and that represents Haman's hat. It is usually filled with poppy, seed, or fruit filling. Haman is the villain in the book of Esther, also known as the *Megillah*.

Hardy A plant that can withstand temperatures at or below freezing.

Hectare A unit of land measure equal to 2.471 acres, or 10,000 square meters.

Huppah The portable canopy under which a Jewish wedding ceremony is held.

Hybrid Offspring of a cross between two plants with different genetic makeups. Hybrids are often sterile and never reproduce truly from seed.

Kabbalah A Jewish mystical philosophy developed during the Middle Ages.

Karpas A vegetable found on the Passover seder plate and used during the ceremony.

Kiddush A ceremonial blessing recited on the Sabbath and holy days.

Kneading The process in bread-making of systematically folding and pressing the dough.

Lulav The name given to the palm branch used with the "Four Species" on Sukkot.

Maror A bitter herb symbolizing the bitter plight of the enslaved Israelites. One of the symbolic foods found on the Passover seder plate.

Menorah The seven-branched candelabrum used on Hanukkah.

Mishloach manot Sending portions of food to friends to celebrate Purim.

Mishnah Legal codification containing the core of the Oral Law.

Mitzvah (pl., *mitzvot*) Literally, a commandment. A religious obligation, it refers to one of the 613 commandments in the Torah.

Mulch Any of a large number of materials, organic or inorganic, that are used to make a protective layer over soil to prevent weed growth, control erosion, maintain an even soil temperature, or conserve moisture.

Nematodes Microscopic, worm-like organisms that can attack all parts of a plant. For an excellent, easy-to-read chapter on nematodes, see *Rodale's Flower Garden Problem Solver*, by Jeff and Liz Ball (New York: MJF Books, 1990)

Node The part of the stem that bears a leaf.

Omer The first sheaf cut during the barley harvest, which was offered in the Temple in Jerusalem on the second day of Passover.

Open-pollinated   Plant varieties produced by natural cross-pollination of parent varieties. They produce true-to-type seeds.

Pita   A flat, round Middle Eastern bread with a pocket that can be filled to make a sandwich.

Pollen   Dustlike grains produced by flowers, containing male sex cells.

Pollination   The transfer of pollen from the anthers of one flower to the receptive stigma of the same or a different flower.

Pruning   Pinching, thinning, heading, or shearing plants to direct growth, promote flowering or fruiting, improve health or appearance, or avoid obstructions.

Puree   A thick liquid or pulp prepared from cooked vegetables or fruit.

Sechach   The roof covering of the *sukkah,* the booth built on the holiday of Sukkot.

Seder   Literally means "order." The ritual meal for the celebration of Passover, Shabbat, and other holy days.

Sephardim   Jews whose origin is Spain. Today the term includes Jews from North Africa and countries around the Mediterranean.

Shehecheyanu   A blessing.

Shivat haminim   The seven varieties of plants mentioned in the Bible to illustrate the richness of the Land of Israel.

Sift   To pass flour and/or other dry ingredients through a sieve.

Sub-tropical   A plant that can tolerate more cold than a tropical plant but cannot withstand freezing temperatures.

Sucker   A fast-growing, upright secondary branch arising from roots, crown, or main branches.

Sukkot   The fall harvest festival.

Spur   Short, fruit-bearing branch of some fruit trees.

Tuber   The enlarged portion of an underground stem, such as a potato.

Variety   A group of plants of one species with particular characteristics in common not shared by other plants of the same species.

SOURCES OF SEEDS, PLANTS, AND OTHER SUPPLIES

When you begin collecting seeds and plants for your Jewish garden, you should order only from legitimate retail outlets. The United States Department of Agriculture strictly forbids bringing in any kind of plant material from overseas. This pertains to material such as plants, seeds, cuttings, and fruit.

Burpee Seed Company
032763 Burpee Building
Warminster, PA 18947
Telephone: (800) 888-1447
Fax: (800) 487-5530
www.burpee.com

Burpee offers two different catalogs. One is their annual general catalog of vegetable and flower seeds. The other is a special catalog with just heirloom varieties. You can order some of their more popular items on-line, but to see their full line of products you will have to request their free catalog. The website offers a question and answer service for all your gardening questions. They promise to respond via e-mail within forty-eight hours.

Cooks Garden
P.O. Box 535
Landenberg, VT 05148
Telephone: (800) 457-9703
Telephone (Canada): (802) 824-3400
Fax: (800) 457-9705
Fax (Canada): (802) 824-3027
www.cooksgarden.com

This attractive, easy-to-read catalog has a large number of vegetables and flowers. Many of them are hard to find, or unusual varieties. They have a particularly large selection of salad greens. The catalog also has herbs, including a large selection of regular and scented basil. Kitchen supplies, garden supplies, and books can also be found in the catalog.

Edible Landscaping
361 Spirit Ridge Lane
P.O. Box 77
Afton, VA 22920
Telephone: (800) 524-4156
www.eat-it.com
E-mail: el@cstone.com

Large selection of fruits (including citrus), nuts, and berries. Though their catalog does include a number of different fig varieties, you should ask to also receive their separate fig sheet, which has a much more extensive listing of varieties.

Johnny's Selected Seeds
Foss Hill Road
Albion, ME 04910
Telephone: (207) 437-4357
Fax: (207) 437-2165
www.johnnyseeds.com

Heavily illustrated and descriptive catalog with many flowers, vegetables, and herbs. (Sixteen varieties of basil are offered!) Excellent growing instructions are included for many of the plants. There is also a section of grains, including several varieties of wheat. Kitchen supplies, garden tools, and books can also be found in the catalog.

Lavender Lane
7337 #1 Roseville Road
Sacramento, CA 95842
Telephone: (888) 593-4400
www.choicemall.com/lavenderln/
E-mail: donna@rcip.com

Offers large and small self-sealing empty tea bags.

J. E. Miller Nurseries, Inc.
5060 West Lake Road
Canandaigua, NY 14424
Telephone: (800) 836-9630
www.millernurseries.com
E-mail: jmiller@millernurseries.com

Large selection of cold-hardy fruits, berries, and nuts, including fifty-seven varieties of apples. Their website advertises special offers, but you cannot order on-line.

Park Seed
1 Parkton Avenue
Greenwood, SC 29647-0001
Telephone: (800) 845-3369
Fax: (800) 275-9941
www.parkseed.com
E-mail: gardener@parkseed.com (questions);
orders@parkseed.com (orders)

Lavishly-illustrated catalog with many vegetables and flowers. Many of the selections are new hybrid varieties offered only by Park Seed. In addition to seed the catalog also offers some herbs as small plants. Park also distributes Park's Countryside Gardens—a catalog of perennials and flowering shrubs.

San Francisco Herb Company
Telephone: (800) 227-4530
www.sfherb.com
E-mail: comments@SFHerb.com

Selection of herbs, spices, tea, botanicals, and large and small-sized self-sealing empty tea bags.

Santa Barbara Heirloom Nursery
Suite 1
P.O. Box 4235
Santa Barbara, CA 93140
Telephone: (805) 968-5444
Fax: (805) 562-1248
www.heirloom.com/heirloom/
E-mail: heirloom@heirloom.com

This nursery offers a selection of organically grown vegetable and herb seedlings. The general plant categories are herbs (medicinal and culinary), vegetables, and edible flowers.

Seeds of Change
P.O. Box 15700
Santa Fe, NM 87506-5700
Telephone: (888) 762-7333
Fax: (888) 329-4762
www.seedsofchange.com

Large selection of open-pollinated vegetables and flowers, including heirloom varieties. Many of the selections are hard-to-find varieties of vegetables and herbs from around the world. The extensive collection of potatoes covers tubers in blue, purple, red, white, and yellow.

Shepherd's Garden Seeds
30 Irene Street
Torrington, CT 06790
Telephone: (860) 482-3638
Fax: (860) 482-0532
www.shepherdseeds.com

This catalog of over one hundred pages offers flower and vegetable seeds from around the world, including a number of vegetables bred in Israel. The section for flowers includes separate collections of fragrant flowers, flowers that attract hummingbirds and butterflies, and evening blooming flowers, among others. There is also an extensive listing of vegetables and herbs as well as kitchen utensils and garden tools.

Southern Perennials & Herbs
98 Bridges Road
Tylertown, MS 39667-9338
Telephone: (800) 774-0079
Fax: (601) 684-3729
www.s-p-h.com

If you're looking for a selection of plants suited to the climate of the deep south, this catalog is worth checking out. It has a section of perennials, herbs (including a large selection of mints), vines, and ornamental grasses.

Stark Brothers Nursery & Orchards
P.O. Box 10
Louisiana, MO 63353-0010
Telephone: (800) 478-2759
www.starkbros.com
E-mail: starkbros@msn.com

This company has a large selection of fruit and nut trees, grapes, and berries. They are primarily for temperate climates. The on-line catalog has an illustration of each item, a description, and price. You can order on-line or you can request their free catalog. There is also extensive growing information on such topics as planting, pruning, and harvesting.

Well-Sweep Herb Farm
205 Mt. Bethel Road
Port Murray, NJ 07865
Telephone: (908) 852-5390

Extensive selection of herb plants, seeds, and herb products, many not available from other sources. The majority of listings have very little description, but if you know what you want, this is an excellent source. They have more than thirty kinds of basil and over one hundred varieties of scented geraniums.

SUGGESTED ADDITIONAL READING

Bernstein, Ellen, ed. *Ecology & the Jewish Spirit: Where Nature and the Sacred Meet.* Woodstock, Vt.: Jewish Lights Publishing, 1997.

Chaim, Raphael. *A Feast of History: Passover through the Ages as a Key to Jewish Experience.* New York: Simon & Schuster, 1972.

Coombs, Duncan, et al. *The Complete Book of Pruning.* London: Ward Lock, 1994.

Greenberg, Irving. *The Jewish Way: Living the Holidays.* New York: Touchstone, 1993.

Heschel, Abraham Joshua. *The Sabbath.* New York: Farrar, Straus & Giroux, 1975.

Klagsbrun, Francine. *Jewish Days: A Book of Jewish Life and Culture around the Year.* New York: Farrar, Straus & Giroux, 1996.

Kushner, Lawrence. *The Book of Words: Talking Spiritual Life, Living Spiritual Talk.* Woodstock, Vt.: Jewish Lights Publishing, 1990.

Lerner, Michael. *Jewish Renewal: A Path to Healing and Transformation.* New York: G. P. Putnam's Sons, 1994.

Marcin, Marietta Marshall. *The Herbal Tea Garden: Planning, Planting, Harvesting & Brewing.* Pownal, Vt.: Storey Communications, 1993.

Ogden, Shepherd and Ellen. *The Cook's Garden: Growing and Using the Best-Tasting Vegetable Varieties.* Emmaus, Pa.: Rodale Press, 1989.

Rogers, Marc. *Saving Seeds: The Gardener's Guide to Growing and*

Storing Vegetables and Flower Seeds. Pownal, Vt.: Storey Communications, 1990.

Sasso, Sandy Eisenberg. *A Prayer for the Earth: The Story of Naamah, Noah's Wife.* Woodstock, Vt.: Jewish Lights Publishing, 1996.

Strassfield, Michael. *The Jewish Holidays: A Guide and Commentary.* New York: Harper & Row, 1985.

BIBLIOGRAPHY

Alon, Azaria. *Natural History of the Land of the Bible.* Garden City, N.Y.: Doubleday, 1978.

Ball, Jeff and Liz. *Rodale's Flower Garden Problem Solver.* New York: MJF Books, 1990.

Borowski, Oded. *Agriculture in Iron Age Israel: The Evidence from Archaeology and the Bible.* Winoma Lake, Ind.: Eisenbrauns, 1987.

Encyclopaedia Judaica. Jerusalem: Keter Publishing House, 1971.

Kitov, Eliyahu. *The Book of Our Heritage: The Jewish Year and Its Days of Significance.* New York: Feldheim Publishers, 1978.

Schwartz, Howard and Anthony Rudolf. *Voices within the Ark.* New York: Pushcart Press, 1980.

About JEWISH LIGHTS Publishing

People of all faiths and backgrounds yearn for books that attract, engage, educate and spiritually inspire.

Our principal goal is to stimulate thought and help all people learn about who the Jewish People are, where they come from, and what the future can be made to hold. While people of our diverse Jewish heritage are the primary audience, our books speak to people in the Christian world as well and will broaden their understanding of Judaism and the roots of their own faith.

We bring to you authors who are at the forefront of spiritual thought and experience. While each has something different to say, they all say it in a voice that you can hear.

Our books are designed to welcome you and then to engage, stimulate and inspire. We judge our success not only by whether or not our books are beautiful and commercially successful, but by whether or not they make a difference in your life.

We at Jewish Lights take great care to produce beautiful books that present meaningful spiritual content in a form that reflects the art of making high quality books. Therefore, we want to acknowledge those who contributed to the production of this book.

PRODUCTION
Bronwen Battaglia

EDITORIAL & PROOFREADING
Jennifer Goneau & Martha McKinney

COVER DESIGN
Molly Cook Field

COVER PRINTING
Phoenix Color Corp., Taunton, Massachusetts

PRINTING AND BINDING
Royal Book, Norwich, Connecticut

New from Jewish Lights

"WHO IS A JEW?"
Conversations, Not Conclusions
by *Meryl Hyman*

Who is "Jewish enough" to be considered a Jew? And by whom?

Meryl Hyman courageously takes on this timely and controversial question to give readers the perspective necessary to draw their own conclusions. With the skill of a seasoned journalist, she weaves her own life experiences into this complex and controversial story. Profound personal questions of identity are explored in conversations with Jew and non-Jew in the U.S., Israel and England. *"Who Is a Jew?"* is a book for those who seek to understand the issue, and for those who think they already do.

6" x 9", 272 pp. HC, ISBN 1-879045-76-1 **$23.95**

THE JEWISH GARDENING COOKBOOK
Growing Plants & Cooking for Holidays & Festivals
by *Michael Brown*

Through gardening and cooking for holiday and festival use, we can recover and discover many exciting aspects of Judaism to nourish both the mind and the spirit. Whether you garden in an herb garden, on a city apartment windowsill or patio, or on an acre, with the fruits and vegetables of your own gardening labors, the traditional repasts of Jewish holidays and celebrations can be understood in many new ways!

Gives easy-to-follow instructions for raising foods that have been harvested since ancient times. Provides carefully selected, tasty and easy-to-prepare recipes using these traditional foodstuffs for holidays, festivals, and life cycle events. Clearly illustrated with more than 30 fine botanical illustrations. For beginner and professional alike.

6" x 9", 224 pp. HC, ISBN 1-58023-004-0 **$21.95**

WANDERING STARS
An Anthology of Jewish Fantasy & Science Fiction
Edited by *Jack Dann;* with an Introduction by *Isaac Asimov*

Jewish science fiction and fantasy? *Yes!*

Here is the distinguished list of contributors to *Wandering Stars*, originally published in 1974 and the only book of its kind, anywhere: Bernard Malamud, Isaac Bashevis Singer, Isaac Asimov, Robert Silverberg, Harlan Ellison, Pamela Sargent, Avram Davidson, Geo. Alec Effinger, Horace L. Gold, Robert Sheckley, William Tenn and Carol Carr. Pure enjoyment. We laughed out loud reading it. A 25th Anniversary Classic Reprint.

"It is delightful and deep, hilarious and sad." —*James Morrow, author,* Towing Jehovah

6" x 9", 272 pp. Quality Paperback, ISBN 1-58023-005-9 **$16.95**

THE ENNEAGRAM AND KABBALAH
Reading Your Soul
by *Rabbi Howard A. Addison*

What do the Enneagram and *Kabbalah* have in common? Together, can they provide a powerful tool for self-knowledge, critique, and transformation?

How can we distinguish between acquired personality traits and the essential self hidden underneath?

6" x 9", 176 pp. Quality Paperback Original, ISBN 1-58023-001-6 **$15.95**

Spirituality

MEDITATION FROM THE HEART OF JUDAISM
Today's Teachers Share Their Practices, Techniques, and Faith
Edited by *Avram Davis*

A "how-to" guide for both beginning and experienced meditators, it will help you start meditating or help you enhance your practice.

Twenty-two masters of meditation explain why and how they meditate. *A detailed compendium of the experts' "Best Practices"* offers practical advice and starting points.

"A treasury of meditative insights and techniques....Each page is a meditative experience that brings you closer to God."
> —*Rabbi Shoni Labowitz, author of* Miraculous Living: A Guided Journey in Kabbalah through the Ten Gates of the Tree of Life

6" x 9", 256 pp. Hardcover, ISBN 1-879045-77-X **$21.95**

SELF, STRUGGLE & CHANGE
Family Conflict Stories in Genesis and Their Healing Insights for Our Lives
by *Norman J. Cohen*

How do I find greater wholeness in my life and in my family's life?

The people described by the biblical writers of Genesis were in situations and relationships very much like our own. We identify with them. Their stories still speak to us because they are about the same problems we deal with every day. Here a modern master of biblical interpretation brings us greater understanding of the ancient text and of ourselves in this intriguing re-telling of conflict between husband and wife, father and son, brothers, and sisters.

"Delightfully written...rare erudition, sensitivity and insight." —*Elie Wiesel*

6" x 9", 224 pp. Quality Paperback, ISBN 1-879045-66-4 **$16.95**; HC, ISBN-19-2 **$21.95**

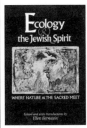

ECOLOGY & THE JEWISH SPIRIT
Where Nature & the Sacred Meet
Edited and with Introductions by *Ellen Bernstein*

What is nature's place in our spiritual lives?

A focus on nature is part of the fabric of Jewish thought. Here, experts bring us a richer understanding of the long-neglected themes of nature that are woven through the biblical creation story, ancient texts, traditional law, the holiday cycles, prayer, *mitzvot* (good deeds), and community.

For people of all faiths, all backgrounds, this book helps us to make nature a sacred, spiritual part of our own lives.

"A great resource for anyone seeking to explore the connection between their faith and caring for God's good creation, our environment."
> —*Paul Gorman, Executive Director, National Religious Partnership for the Environment*

6" x 9", 288 pp. HC, ISBN 1-879045-88-5 **$23.95**

ISRAEL—A SPIRITUAL TRAVEL GUIDE
A Companion for the Modern Jewish Pilgrim
by *Rabbi Lawrence A. Hoffman*

Be spiritually prepared for your journey to Israel.

A Jewish spiritual travel guide to Israel, helping today's pilgrim tap into the deep spiritual meaning of the ancient—and modern—sites of the Holy Land. Combines in quick reference format ancient blessings, medieval prayers, biblical and historical references, and modern poetry. The only guidebook that helps readers to prepare spiritually for the occasion. More than a guide book: It is a spiritual map.

"To add spiritual dimension to your journey, pack this extraordinary new guidebook to Israel. I'll be bringing it on my next visit."
> —*Gabe Levenson, travel columnist for* The New York Jewish Week

4 3/4" x 10 1/8", 256 pp. Quality Paperback Original, ISBN 1-879045-56-7 **$18.95**

Spirituality

HOW TO BE A PERFECT STRANGER, In 2 Volumes
A Guide to Etiquette in Other People's Religious Ceremonies
Edited by *Stuart M. Matlins & Arthur J. Magida*

BEST REFERENCE BOOK OF THE YEAR

"A book that belongs in every living room, library and office!"

Explains the rituals and celebrations of America's major religions/denominations, helping an interested guest to feel comfortable, participate to the fullest extent possible, and avoid violating anyone's religious principles. Answers practical questions from the perspective of *any* other faith.

•Award Winner•

VOL. 1: America's Largest Faiths

VOL. 1 COVERS: Assemblies of God • Baptist • Buddhist • Christian Science • Churches of Christ • Disciples of Christ • Episcopalian • Greek Orthodox • Hindu • Islam • Jehovah's Witnesses • Jewish • Lutheran • Methodist • Mormon • Presbyterian • Quaker • Roman Catholic • Seventh-day Adventist • United Church of Christ

6" x 9", 432 pp. Hardcover, ISBN 1-879045-39-7 **$24.95**

VOL. 2: Other Faiths in America

VOL. 2 COVERS: African American Methodist Churches • Baha'i • Christian and Missionary Alliance • Christian Congregation • Church of the Brethren • Church of the Nazarene • Evangelical Free Church of America • International Church of the Foursquare Gospel • International Pentecostal Holiness Church • Mennonite/Amish • Native American • Orthodox Churches • Pentecostal Church of God • Reformed Church of America • Sikh • Unitarian Universalist • Wesleyan

6" x 9", 416 pp. HC, ISBN 1-879045-63-X **$24.95**

GOD & THE BIG BANG
Discovering Harmony Between Science & Spirituality
by *Daniel C. Matt*

Mysticism and science: What do they have in common? How can one enlighten the other? By drawing on modern cosmology and ancient Kabbalah, Matt shows how science and religion can together enrich our spiritual awareness and help us recover a sense of wonder and find our place in the universe.

"This poetic new book...helps us to understand the human meaning of creation."
—*Joel Primack, leading cosmologist, Professor of Physics, University of California, Santa Cruz*

•Award Winner•

6" x 9", 216 pp. Quality Paperback, ISBN 1-879045-89-3 **$16.95** HC, ISBN-48-6 **$21.95**

MINDING THE TEMPLE OF THE SOUL
Balancing Body, Mind, & Spirit through Traditional Jewish Prayer, Movement, & Meditation
by *Tamar Frankiel* and *Judy Greenfeld*

This new spiritual approach to physical health introduces readers to a spiritual tradition that affirms the body and enables them to reconceive their bodies in a more positive light. Relying on Kabbalistic teachings and other Jewish traditions, it shows us how to be more responsible for our own psychological and physical health. Focuses on the discipline of prayer, simple Tai Chi–like exercises and body positions, and guides the reader throughout, step-by-step, with diagrams, sketches and meditations.

7"x 10", 184 pp. Quality Paperback Original, illus., ISBN 1-879045-64-8 **$16.95**

Audiotape of the Blessings, Movements & Meditations (60-min. cassette) **$9.95**
Videotape of the Movements & Meditations (46-min. VHS) **$20.00**

Spirituality

MY PEOPLE'S PRAYER BOOK
Traditional Prayers, Modern Commentaries
Vol. 1—The *Sh'ma* and Its Blessings
Vol. 2—The *Amidah*
Edited by *Rabbi Lawrence A. Hoffman*

Provides a diverse and exciting commentary to the traditional liturgy, written by 10 of today's most respected scholars and teachers from all perspectives of the Jewish world.

With 7 volumes published semiannually until completion of the series, this stunning work enables all of us to be involved in a personal dialogue with God, history and tradition through the heritage of the prayer book.

"This book engages the mind and heart....It challenges one's assumptions at whatever level of understanding one brings to the text." —*Jewish Herald-Voice*

Vol. 1: 7" x 10", 168 pp. HC, ISBN 1-879045-79-6 **$19.95**
Vol. 2: 7" x 10", 200 pp. (est.) HC, ISBN 1-879045-80-X **$21.95**

FINDING JOY
A Practical Spiritual Guide to Happiness
by *Dannel I. Schwartz* with *Mark Hass*

Searching for happiness in our modern world of stress and struggle is common; *finding* it is more unusual. This guide explores and explains how to find joy through a time-honored, creative—and surprisingly practical—approach based on the teachings of Jewish mysticism and Kabbalah.

"Lovely, simple introduction to Kabbalah....a singular contribution...."
—*American Library Association's* Booklist

•AWARD WINNER•

6" x 9", 192 pp. Quality PB, ISBN 1-58023-009-1 **$14.95** HC, ISBN 1-879045-53-2 **$19.95**

THE DEATH OF DEATH
Resurrection and Immortality in Jewish Thought
by *Neil Gillman*

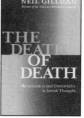

Noted theologian Neil Gillman explores the original and compelling argument that Judaism, a religion often thought to pay little attention to the afterlife, not only offers us rich ideas on the subject—but delivers a deathblow to death itself. By exploring Jewish thought about death and the afterlife, this fascinating work presents us with challenging new ideas about our lives.

"Enables us to recover our tradition's understanding of the afterlife and breaks through the silence of modern Jewish thought on immortality.... A work of major •AWARD WINNER• significance."

—*Rabbi Sheldon Zimmerman, President, Hebrew Union College–Jewish Institute of Religion*

6" x 9", 336 pp., HC, ISBN 1-879045-61-3 **$23.95**

THE EMPTY CHAIR: FINDING HOPE & JOY
Timeless Wisdom from a Hasidic Master,
Rebbe Nachman of Breslov
Adapted by Moshe Mykoff and the Breslov Research Institute

A "little treasure" of aphorisms and advice for living joyously and spiritually today, written 200 years ago, but startlingly fresh in meaning and use. Challenges and helps us to move from stress and sadness to hope and joy.

Teacher, guide and spiritual master—Rebbe Nachman provides vital words of inspiration and wisdom for life today for people of any faith, or of no faith.

•AWARD WINNER•

"For anyone of any faith, this is a book of healing and wholeness, of being alive!"
— *Bookviews*

4" x 6", 128 pp., 2-color text, Deluxe Paperback, ISBN 1-879045-67-2 **$9.95**

Spirituality

GOD WAS IN THIS PLACE & I, i DID NOT KNOW
Finding Self, Spirituality & Ultimate Meaning
by Lawrence Kushner

Who am I? Who is God? Kushner creates inspiring interpretations of Jacob's dream in Genesis, opening a window into Jewish spirituality for people of all faiths and backgrounds.

In this fascinating blend of scholarship, imagination, psychology and history, seven Jewish spiritual masters ask and answer fundamental questions of human experience.

"Rich and intriguing."
—*M. Scott Peck, M.D., author of* The Road Less Traveled *and other books*

6" x 9", 192 pp. Quality Paperback, ISBN 1-879045-33-8 **$16.95**

THE RIVER OF LIGHT
Spirituality, Judaism, Consciousness
by Lawrence Kushner

A "manual" for all spiritual travelers who would attempt a spiritual journey in our times. Taking us step by step, Kushner allows us to discover the meaning of our own quest: "to allow the river of light—the deepest currents of consciousness—to rise to the surface and animate our lives."

"Philosophy and mystical fantasy....Anybody—Jewish, Christian, or otherwise...will find this book an intriguing experience."
—*Kirkus Reviews*

6" x 9", 180 pp. Quality Paperback, ISBN 1-879045-03-6 **$14.95**

GODWRESTLING—ROUND 2
Ancient Wisdom, Future Paths
by *Arthur Waskow*

This 20th-anniversary sequel to a seminal book of the Jewish renewal movement deals with spirituality in relation to personal growth, marriage, ecology, feminism, politics, and more. Including new chapters on recent issues and concerns, Waskow outlines original ways to merge "religious" life and "personal" life in our society today.

BEST RELIGION BOOK OF THE YEAR

•AWARD WINNER• "A delicious read and a soaring meditation."
—*Rabbi Zalman M. Schachter-Shalomi*

"Vivid as a novel, sharp, eccentric, loud....An important book for anyone who wants to bring Judaism alive."
—*Marge Piercy*

6" x 9", 352 pp. Quality Paperback, ISBN 1-879045-72-9 **$18.95** HC, ISBN-45-1 **$23.95**

BEING GOD'S PARTNER
How to Find the Hidden Link Between Spirituality and Your Work
by *Jeffrey K. Salkin* Introduction by *Norman Lear*

Will challenge people of every denomination to reconcile the cares of work and soul. A groundbreaking book about spirituality and the work world, from a Jewish perspective. Helps the reader find God in the ethical striving and search for meaning in the professions and in business and offers practical suggestions for balancing your professional life and spiritual self.

"This engaging meditation on the spirituality of work is grounded in Judaism but is relevant well beyond the boundaries of that tradition."
—*Booklist (American Library Association)*

6" x 9", 192 pp. Quality Paperback, ISBN 1-879045-65-6 **$16.95** HC, ISBN-37-0 **$19.95**

Spirituality—The Kushner Series

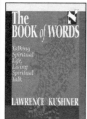

INVISIBLE LINES OF CONNECTION
Sacred Stories of the Ordinary
by *Lawrence Kushner*

Through his everyday encounters with family, friends, colleagues and strangers, Kushner takes us deeply into our lives, finding flashes of spiritual insight in the process. This is a book where literature meets spirituality, where the sacred meets the ordinary, and, above all, where people of all faiths, all backgrounds can meet one another and themselves.

•AWARD WINNER•
"Does something both more and different than instruct—it inspirits. Wonderful stories, from the best storyteller I know."
— *David Mamet*

5 1/2" x 8 1/2", 160 pp. Quality Paperback, ISBN 1-879045-98-2 **$15.95** HC, -52-4 **$21.95**

HONEY FROM THE ROCK
An Easy Introduction to Jewish Mysticism
by *Lawrence Kushner*

"Quite simply the easiest introduction to Jewish mysticism you can read."

An introduction to the ten gates of Jewish mysticism and how it applies to daily life.

"Captures the flavor and spark of Jewish mysticism. . . . Read it and be rewarded." —*Elie Wiesel*

6" x 9", 168 pp. Quality Paperback, ISBN 1-879045-02-8 **$14.95**

THE BOOK OF WORDS
Talking Spiritual Life, Living Spiritual Talk
by *Lawrence Kushner*

In the incomparable manner of his extraordinary *The Book of Letters*, Kushner now lifts up and shakes the dust off primary religious words we use to describe the spiritual dimension of life. For each word Kushner offers us a startling, moving and insightful explication, and pointed readings from classical Jewish sources that further illuminate the concept. He concludes with a short exercise that helps unite the spirit of the word with our actions in the world.

"This is a powerful and holy book."
—*M. Scott Peck, M.D., author of* The Road Less Traveled *and other books*

"What a delightful wholeness of intellectual vigor and meditative playfulness, and all in a tone of gentleness that speaks to this gentile."
—*Rt. Rev. Krister Stendahl, formerly Dean, Harvard Divinity School/Bishop of Stockholm*

6" x 9", 152 pp. 2-color text, Quality PB ISBN 1-58023-020-2 **$16.95**; HC, ISBN 1-879045-35-4 **$21.95**

THE BOOK OF LETTERS
A Mystical Hebrew Alphabet
by *Rabbi Lawrence Kushner*

In calligraphy by the author. Folktales about and exploration of the mystical meanings of the Hebrew Alphabet. Open the old prayerbook-like pages of *The Book of Letters* and you will enter a special world of sacred tradition and religious feeling. Rabbi Kushner draws from ancient Judaic sources, weaving talmudic commentary, Hasidic folktales, and kabbalistic mysteries around the letters.

"A book which is in love with Jewish letters."
— *Isaac Bashevis Singer* (לז)

•AWARD WINNER•

• **Popular Hardcover Edition** 6"x 9", 80 pp. HC, two colors, inspiring new Foreword. ISBN 1-879045-00-1 **$24.95**
• **Deluxe Gift Edition** 9"x 12", 80 pp. HC, four-color text, ornamentation, in a beautiful slipcase. ISBN 1-879045-01-X **$79.95**
• **Collector's Limited Edition** 9"x 12", 80 pp. HC, gold-embossed pages, hand-assembled slipcase. With silkscreened print. **Limited to 500 signed and numbered copies.** ISBN 1-879045-04-4 **$349.00**

To see a sample page at no obligation, call us

Healing/Recovery/Wellness

Experts Praise *Twelve Jewish Steps to Recovery*

"Recommended reading for people of all denominations."
—*Rabbi Abraham J. Twerski, M.D.*

TWELVE JEWISH STEPS TO RECOVERY
A Personal Guide to Turning from Alcoholism & Other Addictions...Drugs, Food, Gambling, Sex...
by *Rabbi Kerry M. Olitzky & Stuart A. Copans, M.D.*
Preface by *Abraham J. Twerski, M.D.*; Intro. by *Rabbi Sheldon Zimmerman*; "Getting Help" by *JACS Foundation*

A Jewish perspective on the Twelve Steps of addiction recovery programs with consolation, inspiration and motivation for recovery. It draws from traditional sources and quotes from what recovering Jewish people say about their experiences with addictions of all kinds. Inspiring illustrations of the twelve gates of the Old City of Jerusalem introduce each step.

6" x 9", 136 pp. Quality Paperback, ISBN 1-879045-09-5 **$13.95**

Recovery from Codependence: A Jewish Twelve Steps Guide to Healing Your Soul
by Rabbi Kerry M. Olitzky
  6" x 9", 160 pp. Quality Paperback Original, ISBN 1-879045-32-X **$13.95**   HC, ISBN-27-3 **$21.95**

Renewed Each Day: Daily Twelve Step Recovery Meditations Based on the Bible
by Rabbi Kerry M. Olitzky & Aaron Z.
  6" x 9", Quality Paperback Original, **V. I**, 224 pp. **$14.95**   **V. II**, 280 pp. **$16.95**
  Two-Volume Set ISBN 1-879045-21-4 **$27.90**

One Hundred Blessings Every Day: Daily Twelve Step Recovery Affirmations, Exercises for Personal Growth & Renewal Reflecting Seasons of the Jewish Year
by Rabbi Kerry M. Olitzky
  4 1/2" x 6 1/2", 432 pp. Quality Paperback Original, ISBN 1-879045-30-3 **$14.95**

HEALING OF SOUL, HEALING OF BODY
Spiritual Leaders Unfold the Strength and Solace in Psalms
Edited by *Rabbi Simkha Y. Weintraub, CSW, for The Jewish Healing Center*

A source of solace for those who are facing illness, as well as those who care for them. The ten Psalms which form the core of this healing resource were originally selected 200 years ago by Rabbi Nachman of Breslov as a "complete remedy." Today, for anyone coping with illness, they continue to provide a wellspring of strength. Each Psalm is newly translated, making it clear and accessible, and each one is introduced by an eminent rabbi, men and women reflecting different movements and backgrounds. To all who are living with the pain and uncertainty of illness, this spiritual resource offers an anchor of spiritual comfort.

"Will bring comfort to anyone fortunate enough to read it. This gentle book is a luminous gem of wisdom."
—*Larry Dossey, M.D., author of* Healing Words: The Power of Prayer & the Practice of Medicine

6" x 9", 128 pp. Quality Paperback Original, illus., 2-color text, ISBN 1-879045-31-1 **$14.95**

Theology/Philosophy

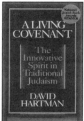

•AWARD WINNER•

A LIVING COVENANT
The Innovative Spirit in Traditional Judaism
by *David Hartman*

WINNER,
National Jewish
Book Award

The Judaic tradition is often seen as being more concerned with uncritical obedience to law than with individual freedom and responsibility. Hartman challenges this approach by revealing a Judaism grounded in a covenant—a relational framework—informed by the metaphor of marital love rather than that of parent-child dependency.

"Jews and non-Jews, liberals and traditionalists will see classic Judaism anew in these pages."
—*Dr. Eugene B. Borowitz, Hebrew Union College–Jewish Institute of Religion*

THE SPIRIT OF RENEWAL
Finding Faith after the Holocaust
by *Edward Feld*

•AWARD WINNER•

Trying to understand the Holocaust and addressing the question of faith after the Holocaust, Rabbi Feld explores three key cycles of destruction and recovery in Jewish history, each of which radically reshaped Jewish understanding of God, people, and the world.

"A profound meditation on Jewish history [and the Holocaust]....Christians, as well as many others, need to share in this story."
—*The Rt. Rev. Frederick H. Borsch, Ph.D., Episcopal Bishop of L.A.*
6" x 9", 224 pp. Quality Paperback, ISBN 1-879045-40-0 **$16.95**

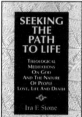

•AWARD WINNER•

SEEKING THE PATH TO LIFE
Theological Meditations On God
and the Nature of People, Love, Life and Death
by *Rabbi Ira F. Stone*

For people who never thought they would read a book of theology—let alone understand it, enjoy it, savor it and have it affect the way they think about their lives. In 45 intense meditations, each a page or two in length, Stone takes us on explorations of the most basic human struggles: Life and death, love and anger, peace and war, covenant and exile.

"A bold book....The reader of any faith will be inspired...."
— *The Rev. Carla V. Berkedal, Episcopal Priest*

6" x 9", 132 pp. Quality Paperback, ISBN 1-879045-47-8 **$14.95** HC, ISBN-17-6 **$19.95**

CLASSICS BY ABRAHAM JOSHUA HESCHEL

The Earth Is the Lord's: The Inner World of the Jew in Eastern Europe
5 1/2" x 8", 112 pp, Quality Paperback, ISBN 1-879045-42-7 **$13.95**

Israel: An Echo of Eternity with new Introduction by Susannah Heschel
5 1/2" x 8", 272 pp, Quality Paperback, ISBN 1-879045-70-2 **$18.95**

A Passion for Truth: Despair and Hope in Hasidism
5 1/2" x 8", 352 pp, Quality Paperback, ISBN 1-879045-41-9 **$18.95**

THEOLOGY & PHILOSOPHY...Other books—Classic Reprints

Aspects of Rabbinic Theology by Solomon Schechter, with a new Introduction by Neil Gillman 6" x 9", 440 pp, Quality Paperback, ISBN 1-879045-24-9 **$18.95**

The Last Trial: On the Legends and Lore of the Command to Abraham to Offer Isaac as a Sacrifice by Shalom Spiegel, with a new Introduction by Judah Goldin
6" x 9", 208 pp, Quality Paperback, ISBN 1-879045-29-X **$17.95**

Judaism and Modern Man: An Interpretation of Jewish Religion by Will Herberg; new Introduction by Neil Gillman 5.5" x 8.5", 336 pp, Quality Paperback, ISBN 1-879045-87-7 **$18.95**

Tormented Master: The Life and Spiritual Quest of Rabbi Nahman of Bratslav by Arthur Green 6" x 9", 408 pp, Quality Paperback, ISBN 1-879045-11-7 **$18.95**

Your Word Is Fire Ed. and trans. with a new Introduction by Arthur Green and Barry W. Holtz 6" x 9", 152 pp, Quality Paperback, ISBN 1-879045-25-7 **$14.95**

Life Cycle

Art of Jewish Living Series for Holiday Observance

THE SHABBAT SEDER
by *Dr. Ron Wolfson*

A concise step-by-step guide designed to teach people the meaning and importance of this weekly celebration, as well as its practices.

Each chapter corresponds to one of ten steps which together comprise the
Shabbat dinner ritual, and looks at the *concepts, objects,* and *meanings*
behind the specific activity or ritual act. The blessings that accompany the
meal are written in both Hebrew and English, and accompanied by English
transliteration. Also included are craft projects, recipes, discussion ideas and
other creative suggestions for enriching the Shabbat experience.

"A how-to book in the best sense...."
—*Dr. David Lieber, President, University of Judaism, Los Angeles*

7" x 9", 272 pp. Quality Paperback, ISBN 1-879045-90-7 **$16.95**

Also available are these helpful companions to *The Shabbat Seder*:
- Booklet of the Blessings and Songs ISBN 1-879045-91-5 $5.00
- Audiocassette of the Blessings DNO3 $6.00
- Teacher's Guide ISBN 1-879045-92-3 $4.95

HANUKKAH
by *Dr. Ron Wolfson*
Edited by *Joel Lurie Grishaver*

Designed to help celebrate and enrich the holiday season, *Hanukkah* discuss-
es the holiday's origins, explores the reasons for the Hanukkah candles and
customs, and provides everything from recipes to family activities.

There are songs, recipes, useful information on the arts and crafts of
Hanukkah, the calendar and its relationship to Christmas time, and games
played at Hanukkah. Putting the holiday in a larger, timely context,
"December Dilemmas" deals with ways in which a Jewish family can cope
with Christmas.

"Helpful for the family that strives to induct its members into the spirituality and joys of
Jewishness and Judaism...a significant text in the neglected art of Jewish family education."
—*Rabbi Harold M. Schulweis, Cong. Valley Beth Shalom, Encino, CA*

7" x 9", 192 pp. Quality Paperback, ISBN 1-879045-97-4 **$16.95**

THE PASSOVER SEDER
by *Dr. Ron Wolfson*

Explains the concepts behind Passover ritual and ceremony in clear, easy-
to-understand language, and offers step-by-step procedures for Passover
observance and preparing the home for the holiday.

Easy-to-Follow Format: Using an innovative photo-documentary technique,
real families describe in vivid images their own experiences with the Passover
holiday. **Easy-to-Read Hebrew Texts:** The Haggadah texts in Hebrew,
English, and transliteration are presented in a three-column format designed
to help celebrants learn the meaning of the prayers and how to read them. **An
Abundance of Useful Information:** A detailed description of how to perform the rituals is included,
along with practical questions and answers, and imaginative ideas for Seder celebration.

"A creative 'how-to' for making the Seder a more meaningful experience."
—*Michael Strassfeld, co-author of* The Jewish Catalog

7" x 9", 336 pp. Quality Paperback, ISBN 1-879045-93-1 **$16.95**

Also available are these helpful companions to *The Passover Seder*:
- Passover Workbook ISBN 1-879045-94-X $6.95
- Audiocassette of the Blessings DNO4 $6.00
- Teacher's Guide ISBN 1-879045-95-8 $4.95

Life Cycle

A HEART OF WISDOM
Making the Jewish Journey from Midlife Through the Elder Years
Edited by *Susan Berrin*

We are all growing older. *A Heart of Wisdom* shows us how to understand our own process of aging—and the aging of those we care about—from a Jewish perspective, from midlife through the elder years.

How does Jewish tradition influence our own aging? How does living, thinking and worshipping as a Jew affect us as we age? How can Jewish tradition help us retain our dignity as we age? Offers insights and enlightenment from Jewish tradition.

"A thoughtfully orchestrated collection of pieces that deal candidly and compassionately with a period of growing concern to us all: midlife through old age."
—Chaim Potok

6" x 9", 384 pp. HC, ISBN 1-879045-73-7 **$24.95**

•AWARD WINNER•

LIFECYCLES
V. 1: Jewish Women on Life Passages & Personal Milestones
Edited and with Introductions by *Rabbi Debra Orenstein*
V. 2: Jewish Women on Biblical Themes in Contemporary Life
Edited and with Introductions by
Rabbi Debra Orenstein and *Rabbi Jane Rachel Litman*

This unique multivolume collaboration brings together over one hundred women writers, rabbis, and scholars to create the first comprehensive work on Jewish life cycle that fully includes women's perspectives.

"Nothing is missing from this marvelous collection. You will turn to it for rituals and inspiration, prayer and poetry, comfort and community. *Lifecycles* is a gift to the Jewish woman in America."
—Letty Cottin Pogrebin, author of Deborah, Golda, and Me:
Being Female and Jewish in America

V. 1: 6" x 9", 480 pp. HC, ISBN 1-879045-14-1, **$24.95**; **V. 2:** 6" x 9", 464 pp. HC, ISBN 1-879045-15-X, **$24.95**

LIFE CYCLE— The Art of Jewish Living Series for Holiday Observance
by Dr. Ron Wolfson

Hanukkah—7" x 9", 192 pp. Quality Paperback, ISBN 1-879045-97-4 **$16.95**

The Shabbat Seder—7" x 9", 272 pp. Quality Paperback, ISBN 1-879045-90-7 **$16.95**; Booklet of Blessings **$5.00**; Audiocassette of Blessings **$6.00**; Teacher's Guide **$4.95**

The Passover Seder—7" x 9", 336 pp. Quality Paperback, ISBN 1-879045-93-1 **$16.95**; Passover Workbook, **$6.95**; Audiocassette of Blessings, **$6.00**; Teacher's Guide **$4.95**

LIFE CYCLE...Other Books

Bar/Bat Mitzvah Basics: A Practical Family Guide to Coming of Age Together
Ed. by Cantor Helen Leneman 6" x 9", 240 pp. Quality Paperback, ISBN 1-879045-54-0 **$16.95**

Embracing the Covenant: Converts to Judaism Talk About Why & How
Ed. and with Intros. by Rabbi Allan L. Berkowitz and Patti Moskovitz
6" x 9", 192 pp. Quality Paperback, ISBN 1-879045-50-8 **$15.95**

The New Jewish Baby Book: Names, Ceremonies, Customs—A Guide for Today's Families by Anita Diamant 6" x 9", 336 pp. Quality Paperback, ISBN 1-879045-28-1 **$16.95**

Putting God on the Guest List, 2nd Ed.: How to Reclaim the Spiritual Meaning of Your Child's Bar or Bat Mitzvah by Rabbi Jeffrey K. Salkin 6" x 9", 224 pp. Quality Paperback, ISBN 1-897045-59-1 **$16.95**; HC, ISBN 1-879045-58-3 **$24.95**

So That Your Values Live On: Ethical Wills & How to Prepare Them
Ed. by Rabbi Jack Riemer & Professor Nathaniel Stampfer
6" x 9", 272 pp. Quality Paperback, ISBN 1-879045-34-6 **$17.95**

Children's Spirituality

A PRAYER FOR THE EARTH
The Story of Naamah, Noah's Wife
For ages 4 and up
by *Sandy Eisenberg Sasso*
Full-color illustrations by *Bethanne Andersen*

NONDENOMINATIONAL, NONSECTARIAN

This new story, based on an ancient text, opens readers' religious imaginations to new ideas about the well-known story of the Flood. When God tells Noah to bring the animals of the world onto the ark, God *also* calls on Naamah, Noah's wife, to save each plant on Earth.

> "A lovely tale....Children of all ages should be drawn to this parable for our times."
>
> —*Tomie dePaola, artist/author of books for children*

• **AWARD WINNER** •

9" x 12", 32 pp. HC, Full-color illus., ISBN 1-879045-60-5 **$16.95**

THE 11TH COMMANDMENT
Wisdom from Our Children
For all ages
by The Children of America

MULTICULTURAL, NONDENOMINATIONAL, NONSECTARIAN

"If there were an Eleventh Commandment, what would it be?"

Children of many religious denominations across America answer this question— in their own drawings and words—in *The 11th Commandment*.

> "Wonderful....This unusual book provides both food for thought and insight into the hopes and fears of today's young."
>
> —*American Library Association's* Booklist

8" x 10", 48 pp. HC, Full-color illus., ISBN 1-879045-46-X **$16.95**

SHARING BLESSINGS
Children's Stories for Exploring the Spirit
of the Jewish Holidays
For ages 6 and up
by *Rahel Musleah* and *Rabbi Michael Klayman*
Full-color illustrations by *Mary O'Keefe Young*

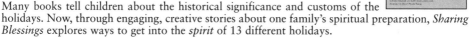

**What is the spiritual message of each of the Jewish holidays?
How do we teach it to our children?**

Many books tell children about the historical significance and customs of the holidays. Now, through engaging, creative stories about one family's spiritual preparation, *Sharing Blessings* explores ways to get into the *spirit* of 13 different holidays.

> "A beguiling introduction to important Jewish values by way of the holidays."
>
> —*Rabbi Harold Kushner, author of* When Bad Things Happen to Good People *and* How Good Do We Have to Be?

7" x 10", 64 pp. HC, Full-color illus., ISBN 1-879045-71-0 **$18.95**

THE BOOK OF MIRACLES
For ages 9–13
A Young Person's Guide to Jewish Spiritual Awareness
by *Lawrence Kushner*

With a Special 10th Anniversary Introduction and all new illustrations by the author.

From the miracle at the Red Sea to the miracle of waking up this morning, this intriguing book introduces kids to a way of everyday spiritual thinking to last a lifetime. Kushner, whose award-winning books have brought spirituality to life for countless adults, now shows young people how to use Judaism as a foundation on which to build their lives.

6" x 9", 96 pp. HC, 2-color illus., ISBN 1-879045-78-8 **$16.95**

Children's Spirituality

For ages 8 and up

BUT GOD REMEMBERED
Stories of Women from Creation to the Promised Land
by *Sandy Eisenberg Sasso*
Full-color illustrations by *Bethanne Andersen*

NONDENOMINATIONAL, NONSECTARIAN

A fascinating collection of four different stories of women only briefly mentioned in biblical tradition and religious texts, but never before explored. Award-winning author Sasso brings to life the intriguing stories of Lilith, Serach, Bityah, and the Daughters of Z, courageous and strong women from ancient tradition. All teach important values through their faith and actions.

•AWARD WINNER•

> "Exquisite....a book of beauty, strength and spirituality."
> —*Association of Bible Teachers*

9" x 12", 32 pp. HC, Full-color illus., ISBN 1-879045-43-5 **$16.95**

IN GOD'S NAME
by *Sandy Eisenberg Sasso*
Full-color illustrations by *Phoebe Stone*

For ages 4 and up

MULTICULTURAL, NONDENOMINATIONAL, NONSECTARIAN

Like an ancient myth in its poetic text and vibrant illustrations, this modern fable about the search for God's name celebrates the diversity and, at the same time, the unity of all the people of the world. Each seeker claims he or she alone knows the answer. Finally, they come together and learn what God's name really is, sharing the ultimate harmony of belief in one God by people of all faiths, all backgrounds.

•AWARD WINNER•

> "I got goose bumps when I read *In God's Name,* its language and illustrations are that moving. This is a book children will love and the whole family will cherish for its beauty and power."
> —*Francine Klagsbrun, author of* Mixed Feelings: Love, Hate, Rivalry, and Reconciliation among Brothers and Sisters

> "What a lovely, healing book!"
> —*Madeleine L'Engle*

> Selected by
> Parent Council, Ltd.™

9" x 12", 32 pp. HC, Full color illus., ISBN 1-879045-26-5 **$16.95**

For ages 4 and up

GOD'S PAINTBRUSH
by *Sandy Eisenberg Sasso*
Full-color illustrations by *Annette Compton*

MULTICULTURAL, NONDENOMINATIONAL, NONSECTARIAN

Invites children of all faiths and backgrounds to encounter God openly in their own lives. Wonderfully interactive, provides questions adult and child can explore together at the end of each episode.

> "An excellent way to honor the imaginative breadth and depth of the spiritual life of the young."
> —*Dr. Robert Coles, Harvard University*

•AWARD WINNER•

11" x 8 1/2", 32 pp. HC, Full-color illus., ISBN 1-879045-22-2 **$16.95**

Also Available!
Teacher's Guide: A Guide for Jewish & Christian Educators and Parents
8 1/2" x 11", 32 pp. PB, ISBN 1-879045-57-5 **$6.95**

AVAILABLE FROM BETTER BOOKSTORES.
TRY YOUR BOOKSTORE FIRST.

Order Information

# of Copies	Book Title / ISBN (Last 3 digits)	$ Amount
_____	_____	_____
_____	_____	_____
_____	_____	_____
_____	_____	_____
_____	_____	_____
_____	_____	_____
_____	_____	_____
_____	_____	_____
_____	_____	_____
_____	_____	_____
_____	_____	_____
_____	_____	_____
_____	_____	_____
_____	_____	_____

For shipping/handling, add $3.50 for the first book, $2.00 each
add'l book (to a max of $15.00) **$ S/H** _____

TOTAL _____

Check enclosed for $_____ *payable to:* JEWISH LIGHTS Publishing

Charge my credit card: ❏ MasterCard   ❏ Visa

Credit Card #_____Expires _____

Signature _____Phone (_____)_____

Your Name _____

Street_____

City / State / Zip _____

Ship To:

Name _____

Street_____

City / State / Zip _____

Phone, fax or mail to: JEWISH LIGHTS Publishing

Sunset Farm Offices, Route 4 • P.O. Box 237 • Woodstock, Vermont 05091
Tel (802) 457-4000   Fax (802) 457-4004   www.jewishlights.com

Credit card orders (800) 962-4544 (9AM–5PM ET Monday–Friday)

Generous discounts on quantity orders. SATISFACTION GUARANTEED. Prices subject to change.

New from Jewish Lights